DETERRENCE AND DEFENSE IN KOREA

Studies in Defense Policy
TITLES PUBLISHED

RALPH N. CLOUGH

DETERRENCE AND DEFENSE IN KOREA

The Role of U.S. Forces

Presented by...

THE BROOKINGS INSTITUTION
Washington, D.C.

Library of Congress Cataloging in Publication Data:

Clough, Ralph N   1916–
   Deterrence and defense in Korea.
   (Studies in defense policy)
   Includes bibliographical references.
   1. United States—Armed Forces—Korea.   2. Korea—
Defenses.   I. Title.   II. Series.
UA26.K6C56   355.03′32′519   75-44466
ISBN 0-8157-1481-5

9 8 7 6 5 4 3 2 1

THE BROOKINGS INSTITUTION is an independent organization devoted to nonpartisan research, education, and publication in economics, government, foreign policy, and the social sciences generally. Its principal purposes are to aid in the development of sound public policies and to promote public understanding of issues of national importance.

The Institution was founded on December 8, 1927, to merge the activities of the Institute for Government Research, founded in 1916, the Institute of Economics, founded in 1922, and the Robert Brookings Graduate School of Economics and Government, founded in 1924.

The Board of Trustees is responsible for the general administration of the Institution, while the immediate direction of the policies, program, and staff is vested in the President, assisted by an advisory committee of the officers and staff. The bylaws of the Institution state: "It is the function of the Trustees to make possible the conduct of scientific research, and publication, under the most favorable conditions, and to safeguard the independence of the research staff in the pursuit of their studies and in the publication of the results of such studies. It is not a part of their function to determine, control, or influence the conduct of particular investigations or the conclusions reached."

The President bears final responsibility for the decision to publish a manuscript as a Brookings book. In reaching his judgment on the competence, accuracy, and objectivity of each study, the President is advised by the director of the appropriate research program and weighs the views of a panel of expert outside readers who report to him in confidence on the quality of the work. Publication of a work signifies that it is deemed a competent treatment worthy of public consideration but does not imply endorsement of conclusions or recommendations.

The Institution maintains its position of neutrality on issues of public policy in order to safeguard the intellectual freedom of the staff. Hence interpretations or conclusions in Brookings publications should be understood to be solely those of the authors and should not be attributed to the Institution, to its trustees, officers, or other staff members, or to the organizations that support its research.

FOREWORD

With the failure of U.S. policy in Indochina and the withdrawal of most U.S. forces from Thailand, public and congressional attention has turned to South Korea—the only remaining portion of the Asian mainland where U.S. forces are stationed. There one American infantry division, backed up by four squadrons of fighter-bombers and tactical nuclear weapons, stands as tangible evidence of the determination of the United States to fulfill its defense commitment to the Republic of Korea. Describing the role of these forces as more political than military, administration spokesmen assert that their continued presence is essential to stability in Northeast Asia. In Congress, however, there are voices calling for their reduction or withdrawal.

In this study Ralph N. Clough analyzes the role of U.S. forces in Korea, assessing their military importance as well as the effect their presence has on relations between the two Koreas. He examines the attitudes of the Soviet Union, China, and Japan toward the U.S. force presence, particularly the effect it has on Japanese views of the U.S. security commitment to Japan. The study proposes that the United States work out with South Korea and Japan a long-term strategy for strengthening South Korean forces and gradually withdrawing U.S. ground forces and tactical nuclear weapons. The author recommends, however, that the United States maintain its air forces in place until improved relations between the two Koreas and evidence of firmer Soviet and Chinese commitment to preserving peace in Korea justify their removal.

Ralph Clough, a former senior fellow at Brookings, is now a Brookings consultant and an adjunct professor of international relations at the American University.

The Brookings Institution expresses its appreciation to General Charles H. Bonesteel, Morton Abramowitz, Robert Scalapino, Michael Armacost,

Daniel O'Donahue, and Donald Alderson for their helpful comments on this study. The military appraisals herein benefited from the work done by William D. White when he was a Brookings research associate. The author is also grateful to his colleagues at Brookings—Henry Owen, Joseph A. Yager, A. Doak Barnett, Barry M. Blechman, and Jeffrey Record—for their support and advice. The manuscript was edited by Elizabeth H. Cross.

The Institution acknowledges the assistance of the Ford Foundation whose grant helps to support its work in defense studies. The views expressed in the study are those of the author and should not be ascribed to those who provided advice and comment, to the Ford Foundation, or to the trustees, officers, or other staff members of the Brookings Institution.

KERMIT GORDON
President

January 1976
Washington, D.C.

CONTENTS

CHAPTER ONE

INTRODUCTION

The sudden collapse of the South Vietnamese government, which had been supported by the United States for over twenty years, has shifted the power balance in Southeast Asia and caused some U.S. allies to have doubts about the reliability of the United States if they should face a military threat. South Korea, like South Vietnam part of a divided country, has been particularly affected. Decisions concerning the future of U.S. forces in South Korea must therefore take account of the changed atmosphere.

South Korea is more important to the United States than South Vietnam because of its close relation to the major U.S. ally in East Asia, Japan, and the impact of what may happen there on the Japanese and their view of the United States. In the aftermath of the events in Indochina, Japanese have been more inclined to question the firmness of the U.S. commitment to the defense of Korea and Japan. Korea is also important because any renewed conflict there would create a serious risk of drawing in the big powers.

Even before the end of the Vietnam War, questions had been raised in Congress about U.S. relations with South Korea. Certain members of Congress and witnesses at congressional hearings argued that the United States was overextended around the world and that U.S. forces in South Korea, as well as in other places, should be reduced, either because the need for them had declined or because the burden of keeping them there was too great.[1] Others criticized the constitutional changes and the repression of the opposition carried out by President Park Chung-hee to maintain himself in power and advocated cutting U.S. military aid if he failed to moderate his repressive measures.[2]

1. See *Our Commitments in Asia*, Hearings before the Subcommittee on East Asian and Pacific Affairs of the House Committee on Foreign Affairs, 93:2 (Government Printing Office, 1974).
2. See *Foreign Assistance Act of 1974*, Report of the Senate Committee on Foreign Relations, 93:2 (GPO, 1974), p. 39.

For some, the failure of U.S. policy in Vietnam strengthens the arguments for early withdrawal of a part or all of the U.S. forces in South Korea; for others, it strengthens the arguments for not disturbing this symbol of U.S. determination to maintain a strong position in the western Pacific. Whichever view one may hold, the new circumstances clearly call for a reexamination of the rationale for continuing to keep U.S. forces in this forward position in Northeast Asia.

When the Korean armistice was signed on July 27, 1953, the two armies facing each other across the truce line were predominantly Chinese in the North and American in the South. The bloody mauling of South Korean divisions by the Chinese in the final battles of the war had demonstrated conclusively that the South Koreans were in no position to hold the line without strong U.S. support. On the other side of the line North Korean forces had been similarly reduced to a secondary position.

Immediately after the armistice, however, the rebuilding of the two Korean forces began. Supplied with large amounts of weapons and other military matériel by their big power allies, Koreans increasingly assumed the responsibility for their own defense. In 1958 Chinese forces withdrew entirely from Korea. Strong U.S. forces remained but were gradually reduced. By 1971, with the withdrawal of one of two remaining U.S. divisions, their number had fallen to around 40,000. American GIs no longer stood guard along the demilitarized zone (DMZ),[3] although the U.S. 2nd Infantry Division was positioned not far behind it to help defend the short, thirty-mile corridor leading from the DMZ to Seoul. Its firepower was augmented by a wing of U.S. fighter-bombers and by tactical nuclear weapons. Thus although the greatly strengthened South Korean forces are now capable of bearing the brunt of any North Korean attack, the American forces constitute a deterrent to intervention by the Chinese from their nearby Manchurian bases.

During the last few years, however, the dramatic improvement in U.S. relations with China has diminished official concern in the United States about possible Chinese military intervention in Korea. Consequently, the official rationale for keeping U.S. forces in South Korea has changed. Former Secretary of Defense James R. Schlesinger testified before a congressional committee in February 1974 that they were there less for the purpose of dealing with possible Chinese support of a North Korean attack

3. With the minor exception of a company-size security force at Panmunjom, where the Military Armistice Commission holds its meetings.

than "to serve as a symbol of America's continued interest in the overall stability of that part of the world during a period of some tension." Although he regarded these forces as a continuing "hedge against military uncertainties," he said that "the political purpose is primary now." He expressed the view that their presence enhanced prospects for negotiation between North and South Korea and added that, depending on how the situation in Korea developed, consideration might be given to transforming them into a mobile reserve, available for use outside Korea.[4] He reaffirmed the political justification at congressional hearings in February 1975, stating that "our forces there serve to contribute to stability on the Korean peninsula and in the area and a precipitous withdrawal would be destabilizing."[5]

The modified official rationale for maintaining some 40,000 U.S. forces in South Korea deserves more probing scrutiny than it has received. Although their primary purpose is now said to be political, the need for forces of this size and composition has not been supported by analysis in depth. Schlesinger may have elaborated his views in the closed sessions that accompanied the open hearings on U.S. forces in Korea, but in a period of strong pressure to reduce U.S. forces overseas there should be fuller public justification of the government's position than has thus far been available.

This study will therefore explore in some detail the reasons for and against continuing the present U.S. force level in South Korea, weighing in particular the risk that U.S. forces might become involved in conflict in Korea against the risks involved in withdrawing them. It will seek to answer a number of questions raised but not adequately answered by official testimony. Why are U.S. forces in South Korea essential to the stability of the region? Must nuclear weapons be stationed in Korea for this purpose? Would a smaller force than the present one be adequate? Could sufficient protection against "military uncertainties" be provided by other means than keeping U.S. forces in Korea? Is there merit in the concept of transforming these forces into a mobile reserve?

Before discussing the political significance of U.S. forces in South Korea, the study will assess the balance of indigenous forces on the Korean peninsula and the possible role of U.S. forces in redressing any imbalance.

---

4. *Department of Defense Appropriations for 1975,* Hearings before the Subcommittee on Department of Defense of the House Committee on Appropriations, 93:2, pt. 1 (GPO, 1974), pp. 581, 583.

5. *Department of Defense Appropriations for 1976,* Hearings before a subcommittee of the House Committee on Appropriations, 94:1, pt. 1 (GPO, 1975), p. 355.

Next, the attitudes of the two Koreas and of the Soviet Union, China, and Japan toward the presence of these outside forces will be analyzed. Finally, in the light of the conclusions reached about the military and political significance of the forces, the probable repercussions to several actions the United States might take, ranging from retaining the present level to total withdrawal, will be evaluated.

CHAPTER TWO

THE MILITARY SIGNIFICANCE
OF U.S. FORCES

On December 31, 1974, U.S. forces stationed in South Korea had a total authorized strength of 42,000.[1] Major units were the 2nd Infantry Division, the 38th Air Defense Artillery Brigade (with Nike-Hercules, Hawk, and Chaparral/Vulcan antiaircraft weapons), the 4th Missile Command (with Sergeant and Honest John missiles), the 3rd Tactical Fighter Wing (with sixty to seventy F-4 aircraft), and the 19th Support Brigade, plus small engineer, transportation, and signal units.

The policy of the U.S. government has been neither to confirm nor to deny that it has nuclear warheads in any particular foreign country. Yet the presence of such weapons in South Korea has been an open secret for some time; in June 1975 then Secretary of Defense Schlesinger stated publicly: "We have deployed in [South] Korea tactical nuclear weapons, as is, I believe, well known."[2]

Several of the weapon systems maintained by the United States in South Korea are capable of delivering either conventional or nuclear explosives: the F-4 fighter-bomber, the Nike-Hercules surface-to-air missiles, the 8-inch and 155 mm howitzers, and the Honest John surface-to-surface missiles. Sergeant missiles carry only nuclear warheads.

Among the "military uncertainties," which Schlesinger referred to as one reason for keeping these forces in Korea, presumably is a residual concern that under some now unforeseen circumstances the Chinese might again become a military threat in Korea. After all, there are fundamental differences between the United States and China on many world issues, and China continues to be a strong backer of North Korea. If relations be-

1. The actual number in Korea may at times fall considerably below this figure. For example, on December 31, 1973, the actual number was 38,000. See *Our Commitments in Asia,* Hearings before the Subcommittee on East Asian and Pacific Affairs of the House Committee on Foreign Affairs, 93:2 (GPO, 1974), p. 183.

2. *Washington Post,* June 21, 1975.

tween the United States and China should deteriorate and tension should rise between the two Koreas, a deterrent to Chinese military intervention in the form of U.S. forces in South Korea might prevent the outbreak of war.

But providing against such a rather remote contingency is no longer an important reason for keeping U.S. forces in South Korea. On the contrary, Schlesinger warned that "abrupt reductions" would have "distressing effects" in China (as well as in Japan and Korea),[3] a political rationale that will be considered further below.

If U.S. forces seem no longer needed in Korea as a deterrent to possible Chinese military intervention, against what other military uncertainties are they a safeguard? The Department of Defense provided an answer in a written response to a question posed by Senator John C. Stennis: "While we believe that South Korean *ground forces* are now adequate for defense against North Korea, we are not so confident of South Korean air defenses and tactical air forces." The department further said that "U.S. support forces in Korea help provide for the timely deployment and support of whatever assistance South Korea might require if attacked—from materiel to combat forces."[4] The reasons for the department's confidence in the defensive capabilities of the South Korean ground forces and its concern about South Korean air defense capabilities can be deduced from a study of the size and equipment of the opposing forces available in published sources, the most comprehensive and recent of which are those contained in *The Military Balance, 1975–1976.*[5]

The Indigenous Force Balance

The military dispositions and capabilities of North and South Korea are greatly influenced by basic geographical factors. Korea is a narrow peninsula, some six hundred miles long but only one hundred to one hundred and fifty miles wide. Much of the terrain is extremely rugged, with moun-

3. *Department of Defense Appropriations for 1975,* Hearings before the Subcommittee on Department of Defense of the House Committee on Appropriations, 93:2, pt. 1 (GPO, 1974), p. 581.

4. *Fiscal Year 1975 Authorization for Military Procurement, Research and Development, and Active Duty, Selected Reserve, and Civilian Personnel Strengths,* Hearings before the Senate Committee on Armed Services, 93:2 (GPO, 1974), p. 1647.

5. London: International Institute for Strategic Studies, 1975, p. 56.

tains rising to nine thousand feet and relatively small flat areas separated from each other by hills or mountain ranges. Seoul, the capital city of South Korea, with 6 million people—almost 20 percent of South Korea's total population—lies only thirty miles south of the demilitarized zone (DMZ) which forms the border with North Korea. South Korea can be supplied only by sea or air, whereas North Korea has a land border with both the USSR and China.

The narrowness of the peninsula and its largely mountainous character do not favor rapid movement by mechanized forces or large numbers of tanks. By forcing an attacker to concentrate his forces in confined areas where they are highly vulnerable to air attack, the terrain confers an advantage on the defense. It is not well suited to air defense, for the hills limit the range of radar, making it possible for enemy aircraft in many places to slip in down a valley below and undetected by the radar screens of defensive units. The short warning period makes it difficult to scramble interceptors in time; thus both sides are vulnerable to preemptive air attacks. Lines of communication, largely dependent on rail transport, offer good opportunities for interdiction. Korea is a country where the decisive military arm is likely to be the infantry if it is adequately backed by mortar and artillery fire and close air support.

The proximity of Seoul to the DMZ (Pyongyang, the North Korean capital, is ninety miles from the DMZ) poses special problems for its defenders. It is accessible from the north by two corridors, one passing through Munsan-ni to the northwest and another through Uijongbu, almost directly north. The short distance precludes defense in depth and the nature of the terrain and the road patterns impede the rapid lateral movement of reserves from east or west into the battle zone. A mass onslaught by North Korean forces through these corridors would be difficult, though not impossible, to halt short of Seoul. Such a blitzkrieg would presumably be immediately preceded by air and commando strikes on airfields, air defense sites, and communications centers, aimed at securing air superiority over the battlefield and sowing confusion in rear areas. To create panic among civilians and further hinder the defense efforts, Seoul itself could be hit by FROG surface-to-surface missiles and by aircraft which could arrive from North Korean airfields with almost no warning.

An attack of this sort might be intended not as the first step in a lengthy campaign to occupy all of South Korea, but rather as an effort to seize crucial territory, strike a crippling blow at the South Korean government, and then gain prompt international backing for a cease-fire in place. Because of Seoul's exposed location, the South Korean government has invested heavily in fortifying the potential invasion corridors, building concrete shelters to protect aircraft from surprise attack, and in other ways raising the odds against a successful blitzkrieg. Further insurance is provided by the presence of the U.S. 2nd Division between Seoul and the DMZ and the availability of U.S. sea and air power.

In any prolonged war, the relative strength of the two ground forces would be critical, and here the South Koreans are in a strong position, especially in the capability to defend against attack. They have a regular army of 560,000 and 20,000 marines whereas North Korea's army totals 410,000. South Korean reserves number 1,000,000 to North Korea's 250,000, and South Korean civilian militia 2,000,000 to North Korea's 1,550,000, although in the latter's highly regimented society reserves and militia may be better trained and in a better state of readiness than those in South Korea. Regular infantrymen in the North are armed with the AK-47 and in the South with the M-16. Soldiers on both sides are tough and well trained. But in numbers alone, a very important factor in any prospective conflict in Korea, South Korea has a significant advantage. Moreover, substantial numbers of South Korean troops have had relatively recent combat experience in the two army divisions and the marine brigade that the Republic of Korea maintained for several years in South Vietnam, although the nature of the fighting there differed from what could be expected in Korea.

The discussion of the relative strength of the ground, sea, and air forces of the two Koreas that follows assumes a conflict in which no outside forces are involved and both sides are initially dependent on existing stocks of weapons and other matériel.

Ground Forces

The South Koreans are listed in table 2-1 as having the same number of medium tanks as the North Koreans. Even if some inaccuracy in the figures is allowed for, it seems unlikely that either side has the substantial advantage in numbers necessary to assure a successful prolonged offensive, particularly in view of the limitations imposed by the terrain on armored warfare. But relative total numbers alone are not conclusive; much would depend on the skill with which the tanks were used, the kind of air support they received, and the types of antitank weapons used by the adversary.

Table 2-1. Active and Reserve Military Personnel and Equipment, South and North Korea, 1975

Branch of service, personnel, and type of equipment	South Korea		North Korea	
	Number	Breakdown or description	Number	Breakdown or description
Total active armed forces	**625,000**		**467,000**	
Army				
Active personnel	**560,000**		**410,000**	
Reserve personnel	1,000,000		250,000	
Surface-to-air missile (SAM) battalions	2	With 8 Hawk and Nike-Hercules batteries	20	With 180 SA-2s
Medium tanks	1,000	M-47s, M-48s, M-60s	1,000	300 T-34s, 700 T-54s/55s and T-59s
Light tanks	0		130	80 PT-76s, 50 T-62s
Artillery pieces	2,000	Up to 203 mm	3,000	Up to 152 mm
Artillery, other	1 battalion	With Honest John surface-to-surface missiles (SSMs)	200	Self-propelled guns
			1,800	Rocket launchers
			12	FROG SSMs
			2,500	Antiaircraft guns
Navy				
Active personnel	**20,000**		**17,000**	
Reserve personnel	33,000		40,000	
Submarines	0		8	4 Soviet W-class, 4 Chinese R-class
Patrol boats	22		18	10 Komars with Styx SSMs; 8 Osas with Styx SSMs
Destroyers	7		0	
Destroyer escorts	9		0	
Minesweepers	10		0	
Subchasers	0		15	
Gunboats	15	Coastal escorts	54	
Torpedo boats	0		90	
Landing ships	20	8 tank, 12 medium	0	
Amphibious craft	60		0	
Marines				
Active personnel	**20,000**		**0**	
Reserve personnel	60,000		0	
Air Force				
Active personnel	**25,000**		**40,000**	
Reserve personnel	35,000		40,000	

Table 2-1 (*continued*)

Branch of service, personnel, and type of equipment	South Korea		North Korea	
	Number	*Breakdown or description*	*Number*	*Breakdown or description*
Combat aircraft	216	70 F-5As, 36 F-4Ds, 100 F-86Fs, 10 RF-5As	588	60 IL-28 bombers, 28 SU-7s, 300 MIG-15s and -17s, 150 MIG-21s, 40 MIG-19s, 10 IL-28 reconnaissance
Paramilitary personnel	2,000,000	Militia	1,500,000	Militia
			50,000	Internal security and border patrol

Source: International Institute for Strategic Studies, *The Military Balance, 1975–1976* (London: IISS 1975), p. 56.

Although the table does not show a complete breakdown of types of medium tanks on each side, it suggests that South Korea has a qualitative advantage. A large part of the North Korean inventory consists of antiquated T-34 tanks, which should be classified as light tanks because they weigh only thirty-two tons and are inferior in both armament and speed to even the aging U.S. M-48s (forty-nine tons), which constitute the bulk of South Korea's tank force. North Korea appears to have no tank comparable to the M-60, which South Korea is now receiving in small numbers. The T-59 medium tanks, which appeared for the first time in the North Korean inventory in 1974, are a Chinese version of the Soviet T-54 and are considered by American military experts to be inferior to the latter in important respects.

It is difficult to judge from the data available which side has the advantage in artillery 105 mm and larger, because there is no breakdown of the numbers of each type. The table suggests, however, that the North Koreans have considerably more artillery pieces than the South Koreans have; this would not be surprising, for Pyongyang's forces are organized and armed on the Soviet pattern and the Soviet Union customarily equips its forces with larger numbers of artillery pieces and mortars than does the United States. North Korean infantry units also have greater firepower in automatic weapons and machine guns than South Korean units, as well as a large number of rocket launchers and two hundred armored, self-propelled guns, weapons that have no counterparts in the South Korean inventory.

The number of artillery "tubes" can be less important, however, than the ability to supply them with ammunition. The North Koreans have an advantage over South Korea in the ability to produce ammunition but would have difficulty keeping forward units supplied in a campaign to occupy South Korea. The North Korean army, like the Soviet army, reflects heavy investment in initial combat power at the expense of the logistic support capabilities required to sustain a prolonged conflict. A force so organized can strike a potent first blow, but against determined resistance that imposed upon it a heavy expenditure of ammunition and equipment, the force might suffer a logistical breakdown.

Despite North Korea's numerical advantages in artillery pieces, the confidence of the U.S. Defense Department in the ability of the South Koreans to defend themselves on the ground suggests that the North Koreans do not have the great advantage over the South Koreans in the larger-caliber, longer-range weapons or the ability to keep them supplied with ammunition that would be needed to exploit an offensive breakthrough.

Naval Forces

The Defense Department statement on the defensive capability of the South Korean forces did not mention naval forces, probably because the navies on both sides are small and would not play an important role in a Korean conflict. The largest vessels are the North Korean submarines and the South Korean destroyers.

The dependence of the South Korean economy on shipping raises the question whether North Korea, with its guided missiles and torpedo boats as well as submarines, might try to impose a naval blockade or mine South Korea's few ports. The relatively weak South Korean air force and navy would find such actions difficult to counter.

The effects of mining or naval blockade would not, however, be confined to Korea. The great majority of ships delivering cargoes to South Korea are non-Korean. Should the North Koreans damage or sink U.S. merchant ships supplying South Korea, the United States would be quite likely to intervene in the conflict. It is difficult to imagine this country permitting its trade with South Korea to be interdicted while the Soviet Union and China were free to trade with North Korea by land. U.S. naval and air power could keep the ports open. Thus the option of mining or naval blockade would virtually be ruled out for North Korea, even in a conflict in which the United States was not initially involved.

Although the South Koreans, with their marine division, could carry out a sizable amphibious assault (a capability the North Koreans do not have), a landing in force behind the main battle line would be contingent on control of both the air and sea in the landing area. The relative weakness of the South Korean air force and navy would preclude such operations.

North Korea has a greater capability than South Korea for infiltrating special forces into rear areas by using fast motorboats and has a larger number of men trained in such operations.

Air Forces

Comparison of the air forces and the air defense weapons of the two sides (see table 2-1) shows why the Defense Department lacks confidence in the ability of South Korean forces alone to cope with the North Korean air force. North Korea has a force of nearly 600 combat aircraft; South Korea has just over 200. Moreover, North Korea has at least sixteen airfields from which to operate while South Korea has only four.

The qualitative superiority of South Korean aircraft somewhat reduces the disparity in overall capability but does not eliminate it. For example, North Korea has no aircraft as modern and versatile as South Korea's F-4s, which can be used for close support of ground forces, bombing of targets far behind enemy lines, or combating enemy aircraft. The 28 SU-7s in North Korea, which are primarily designed to strike ground targets, appear to have been provided by the Soviet Union as a response to the supplying of F-4s to South Korea by the United States. They are about two-thirds the size of the F-4s, however, and are inferior in avionics, range, and payload. Nor are the SU-7s the equal of the F-4s in air combat.

Thus when qualitative differences are taken into account the numerical disparity between the two sides in relatively modern aircraft is less than it appears. Although South Korea has only 70 F-5s[6] and 36 F-4Ds to combat North Korea's 150 MIG-21s, 40 MIG-19s, and 28 SU-7s (106 versus 218), U.S. combat experience in Vietnam suggests that these U.S. aircraft would outperform their Soviet counterparts.[7] The combat exchange ratio

6. Mostly F-5As, but the most recent acquisitions under the modernization program have been the improved F-5E model.
7. William D. White, *U.S. Tactical Air Power: Missions, Forces, and Costs* (Brookings Institution, 1974), p. 66.

for F-4Ds against MIG-21s was between two and three to one. The F-5s are considered roughly equal to the MIG-21s in clear weather and when fighting near their own bases. And the MIG-19s and SU-7s are inferior in air combat to either U.S. aircraft.

In older aircraft, the South Koreans are at a still greater quantitative disadvantage, with only 100 F-86Fs to 300 MIG-15s and -17s. But here the qualitative edge held by South Korea over North Korea is probably greater than in modern aircraft: U.S. pilots flying an earlier model of the F-86 against MIG-15s and -17s in the Korean War outscored them by more than ten to one.

What the overall combat exchange ratio might be is difficult to predict, for much would depend on where the action took place, the types of aircraft used, the skill of the pilots, and the tactics adopted by each side. The better aircraft of the South Koreans would certainly diminish their rather large numerical disadvantage but might not suffice to overcome it.

For the most part air action would take place near the battlefront in the form of close air support for ground forces and air combat as each side struggled to gain control of the air. Neither side would be likely to assign many aircraft to deep penetration missions, in part because both sides protect their aircraft on airfields with shelters, making it difficult for the enemy to inflict heavy losses by surprise attack, but also, and more important, because neither side has aircraft equipped with the electronic penetration devices needed to carry out long-range missions on a scale that would significantly affect enemy capabilities. South Korea's F-4s, although well designed for such missions, are too few to be risked in enemy territory beyond the range of other South Korean fighters. North Korea's IL-28s are old, slow, and highly vulnerable to South Korean interceptors and anti-aircraft defense.

Unless losses were constantly replaced from outside Korea, neither air arm could be expected to have a decisive effect on the outcome of a long war. In a short blitzkrieg against Seoul, however, the probable ability of North Korea to gain local air superiority against South Korean forces fighting alone might determine the outcome. In a longer war, even if the South Korean air force should be virtually destroyed within the first few weeks, it would have taken such a heavy toll of North Korean aircraft that the few remaining would not constitute a formidable military threat. To provide close air support they would have to fly low and expose themselves to South Korea's American-made Hawk missiles and to other surface-to-air weapons.

The data available on surface-to-air defenses indicate that here too the North Koreans probably hold an advantage, primarily because of their large number of antiaircraft guns. None are listed by the International Institute for Strategic Studies for the South Koreans. The South Korean Hawk battalion would partially but not totally overcome this disadvantage. As for North Korea's twenty SAM (surface-to-air missile) battalions with 180 SA-2s and the single South Korean SAM battalion with Nike-Hercules, the imbalance here probably would have little effect on the conflict. High-flying aircraft, which these missile systems are designed to defend against, would not play a significant role in a combat limited to the two Koreas.

This review of the air combat and air defense capabilities of the two sides demonstrates that there is good reason for the doubts expressed by the Defense Department about the air balance between North and South Korea. Even though South Korea's deficiencies in aircraft and air defense weapons might not decisively affect the outcome of a prolonged conflict in a purely military sense, it would be an important psychological victory for North Korea if it gained control of the air so that its remaining aircraft could rove with relative freedom over South Korea.

The Overall Balance

In sum, an assessment of military forces in North and South Korea strongly suggests that neither has the overwhelming military superiority that would give it high confidence in its ability to conquer the other in an all-out struggle in which no outside forces were involved. With the present military balance, however, a blitzkrieg against Seoul might look more promising to the North Koreans if they were no longer deterred by the presence of U.S. forces. Since the Korean forces are fairly evenly matched for an all-out war—any disadvantage of the South Koreans would be further reduced when they were the defenders—the probability is that such a conflict would drag on, with neither side able to win a decisive victory. A war of attrition would soon require resupply of major weapons from outside Korea. Not knowing whether resupply could be counted on and how much would be provided must make the outcome of a conflict still more uncertain.

The foregoing judgments are based on evaluations by American military analysts; South Koreans tend to rate their own military capability lower and that of North Korea higher. They stress the proximity of Seoul

Table 2-2. U.S. Military Assistance for the Modernization of South Korean Ground
and Air Forces, Obligations and Loan Authorizations, Fiscal Years 1971–75
Millions of dollars

Item	1971	1972	1973	1974	1975
Grants	541.2	515.2	338.8	100.6	82.6
Credits or loans	15.0	17.0	24.2	56.7	59.0
Total	556.2	532.2	363.0	157.3	141.6
Cash purchases	0.48	9.0	1.3	56.4	159.8

Sources: For 1971–74, grants and credits from U.S. Agency for International Development, "U.S. Overseas Loans and Grants, Obligations and Loan Authorization, July 1, 1945–June 30, 1974" (AID, 1975; processed); cash purchases from unpublished figures of the U.S. Department of Defense, Defense Assistance Agency, Comptroller. For 1975, all figures from "Security Assistance Program, Foreign Military Sales and Military Assistance Program, Congressional Presentation Document, Fiscal Years 1976 and 197T" (Department of Defense, 1975; processed).

to the DMZ and North Korea's quantitative superiority in artillery and aircraft, as well as its presumed ability to stockpile war matériel received from China and the USSR and to mobilize reserves with great speed from its highly regimented population. Thus they see South Korea, and Seoul in particular, as vulnerable to a blitzkrieg. The greater caution of these evaluations by persons whose homeland is directly threatened is not surprising, and strengthens their argument for more military aid and for retention of U.S. troops in South Korea.

Future Trends

What future trends might upset the rough military balance now existing between North and South Korea? It could be upset if the United States, the Soviet Union, or China were to pour in large amounts of new military equipment, though there is little evidence at present that this is likely. The U.S. modernization program for South Korean ground and air forces, while continuing, is stretching out well beyond the original target date of 1975; it is moving too slowly to change the balance significantly. Table 2-2 shows that U.S. military assistance was large in the first two years of the modernization program, but declined substantially in 1973 and 1974. The probability is that it will decline further in future years.

The Soviet Union also has shown restraint in the supply of modern weapons. China is providing more military equipment to North Korea than in the past,[8] including MIG-21s and T-59 tanks, but it is too much in need

8. In 1972 for the first time it provided more than the USSR. See *Korea and the Philippines: November, 1972,* Staff Report for the Senate Committee on Foreign Relations, 93:1 (GPO, 1973), p. 28.

of more modern weapons for its own forces and too limited in its ability to produce sophisticated major weapon systems to be able to spare large amounts for North Korea. To the extent that the big powers recognize the desirability of not upsetting the military balance in Korea—a subject that will be discussed below—they will continue to exercise restraint in the supply of weapons.

Both Koreas are working toward greater self-sufficiency in military matériel but have a long way to go to be fully self-sufficient. North Korea has for many years produced the AK-47, its standard infantry weapon, and South Korea has recently begun to manufacture the M-16. The capacity of both to produce a variety of other types of minor equipment and consumables for military use is steadily increasing. They are expanding their steel, chemical, machine tool, shipbuilding, and electronics industries, which in time will create a sizable base for the production of naval ships, trucks, communications equipment, mortars, artillery, and ammunition. At present, North Korea has a substantial lead over South Korea in producing military supplies and equipment. Tanks, aircraft, and missiles, however, will probably remain beyond the capability of either Korea for some time.

North Korea, building on its superior industrial legacy from the colonial period, gained an early lead over South Korea in steel production and machine building, but South Korea is closing the gap. In the long run, South Korea will derive considerable advantage from its massive expansion of foreign trade, and the consequent induction on a large scale of foreign capital and technology, that began in the 1960s, when North Korea maintained a high degree of self-sufficiency. Pyongyang's two-way trade in 1970 was only $690 million[9] whereas South Korea's was $2.8 billion.[10] Several years ago North Korea recognized the need to import more foreign technology, but it has been handicapped by a shortage of goods to export. It would have great difficulty adapting its economic system to take advantage of market possibilities in noncommunist countries as South Korea's more open free enterprise system has done so successfully.

The relative military strength of the two Koreas in the future will be significantly affected by their overall economic progress. Consequently,

9. Korean Foreign Trade Association, *North Korean Foreign Trade* (Seoul, 1972), cited in Joong-Koon Lee, "North Korean Trade in Recent Years and the Prospects for North-South Korean Trade," *Journal of Korean Affairs*, vol. 4 (October 1974), p. 19.

10. International Monetary Fund, *Direction of Trade Annual, 1970–74* (International Bank for Reconstruction and Development, 1975), p. 189.

economic development has become an increasingly important element in the competition between them. President Park Chung-hee has stressed the need for rapid economic growth in South Korea so that by the 1980s it will be in a position to negotiate from strength with North Korea on the unification question. South Korea's population of 33 million gives it a fundamental advantage over North Korea with 15 million. Even though its population has been growing in recent years at around 2 percent annually while North Korea's has grown at 3 percent, the gap between the size of the two populations continues to widen. South Korea's gross national product in 1972 was $9.7 billion as against an estimated $5.3 billion for North Korea, and its economic growth from 1963 to 1972 averaged 10.3 percent while North Korea's was 6.5 percent. During the same period North Korea's military budget averaged 14.3 percent of GNP; South Korea's averaged 4 percent. It is significant that in 1972, as North Korea sought to increase its rate of economic growth to compete more effectively with South Korea, it cut military expenditures back to 9.4 percent of GNP.[11]

South Korea's rate of growth probably will not continue to be higher than North Korea's, especially since its economy has been hard hit by the sharp increase in oil prices and world recession: its real growth rate dropped to 8.5 percent in 1974 and is likely to be about 7 percent in 1975. Nevertheless, the gap in absolute terms between its economy and that of North Korea will undoubtedly continue to expand.

These trends imply that time is on the side of South Korea. It is therefore under little pressure to force the unification issue soon. Conversely, North Korea's President Kim Il-sung must feel some urgency to achieve unification before South Korea becomes too strong. But as long as a rough military balance exists he is unlikely to get an opportunity to do so by military means unless severe and prolonged political trouble breaks out in South Korea.

The Military Role of U.S. Forces

If it is assumed that Chinese forces are unlikely to intervene in a renewed conflict between North Korea and South Korea, the purely military justification for the presence of U.S. ground forces in South Korea, either

11. U.S. Arms Control and Disarmament Agency, *World Military Expenditures and Arms Trade, 1963–1973* (GPO, 1975), p. 41.

at present or in the years immediately ahead, is weak. South Korean ground forces are in a strong position to defend against North Korean attack, and the conventional firepower of one U.S. division of some 16,000 men adds only marginally to that available to South Korea's ground forces of 580,000. Of course, tactical nuclear weapons provide a quantum jump in firepower, particularly effective against any massing of North Korean armored forces in an attempt to breach Seoul's defense. But since South Korean ground forces, if provided with adequate close air support, seem capable of holding their own against an attack by North Korean forces alone, U.S. use of nuclear weapons against them would not only risk provoking the Soviet Union to supply tactical nuclear weapons to the North Koreans, but would also carry with it high political costs.

More important from the South Korean viewpoint than the added firepower of U.S. ground forces is the assurance they represent that the United States would fulfill its defense commitment in the event of renewed conflict, thus almost certainly deterring North Korea from launching an attack. Deployment of the U.S. 2nd Division between Seoul and the DMZ ensures its early involvement in any large-scale combat in that sector. Consequently, the division's deterrent effect is doubtless greater than its relatively small size suggests. Forward-based ground forces are better insurance than air units based well behind the front lines since these could be flown out quickly if the United States for any reason decided not to become directly involved in the fighting.

On purely military grounds, the presence of U.S. air units in South Korea is easier to justify than the presence of U.S. ground forces. The sixty F-4s assigned to these units compensate for the relative weakness of the South Korean air force, and their presence also implies that additional U.S. air power, both ground-based and carrier-based, would be brought to bear quickly if needed. So long as these air units are based in South Korea and the readiness of the United States to use them in a conflict remains credible to Pyongyang, North Korea's quantitative advantage in the air over Seoul's forces alone will not encourage hope for a successful military action against the South.

The residual military role of the United States—to redress the imbalance in air power between North and South—could be eliminated by providing South Korea with enough additional aircraft to overcome North Korea's advantage in the air. More airfields in South Korea would also be needed. Were that imbalance corrected, continued maintenance of U.S.

forces in South Korea would have to be justified almost entirely on political grounds.

An important qualification must be made to this assessment. While the Department of Defense judges South Korean ground forces to be capable of holding their own against North Korean attack if supplied with adequate air support, the South Koreans themselves are less confident and we do not know how the North Koreans view the balance. It is impossible to be sure that Kim Il-sung would be deterred by South Korea's present military strength from mounting a blitzkrieg against Seoul if U.S. ground forces pulled out tomorrow. The psychological impact of U.S. withdrawal on the two Koreas might be as important as the weaponry possessed by the two sides in determining both whether North Korea began a conflict and the course that conflict took.

CHAPTER THREE

THE POLITICAL SIGNIFICANCE OF
U.S. FORCES: THE TWO KOREAS

In addition to providing a "hedge against military uncertainties," the presence of U.S. combat forces in South Korea demonstrates that the United States continues to take a deep interest not only in that nation's security but also, more generally, in continued peace in Northeast Asia. Koreans have not forgotten that it was the total withdrawal of U.S. combat forces from South Korea in 1949 and the apparent ebbing of U.S. concern about the country that set the stage for the outbreak of the Korean War in 1950. American forces in Korea strengthen the credibility of the commitment made to the Republic of Korea in the mutual defense treaty of October 1, 1953, and emphasize that, despite the collapse of its position in Indochina and the reduction in the number of its forces elsewhere in Southeast Asia, the United States will not be indifferent to developments that threaten peace in Northeast Asia. Stated in such general terms, the political significance of the U.S. forces in South Korea is self-evident; more difficult to assess is the precise nature and extent of the influence their presence has on the two Koreas and the probable effect of the withdrawal of some or all of them.

North Korean Attitudes

The state most critically affected—other than South Korea—is obviously North Korea. For many years Pyongyang's consistent position has been that U.S. forces should withdraw promptly and totally. Claiming that the U.S. presence has reduced South Korea to a complete colony and military base, the North Koreans condemn Park Chung-hee as a mere puppet, opposed by most of the South Korean people and maintained in power only through U.S. support.[1] In the words of Kim Il-sung, "The occupation of South Korea by the U.S. imperialists and their policy of aggression are the root cause of all our nation's misery, the main obstacle to the reunification of our country and a constant source of war in Korea."[2]

The simplistic North Korean description of the Park Chung-hee government as controlled by U.S. forces in South Korea is doubtless a deliberate exaggeration for propaganda purposes. Nevertheless, the heavy emphasis, which has continued for many years, on the need for the withdrawal of U.S. forces suggests that Kim Il-sung does indeed see them as the chief obstacle to the unification of the Korean peninsula on his terms. Moreover, it would be surprising if he did not also regard them as a potential danger to the security of North Korea.[3] From Kim's viewpoint, the removal of U.S. forces would not only eliminate this threat, but would have other important advantages, such as weakening Park's position and making him more vulnerable to political pressure and paramilitary action. To the extent that U.S. military intervention became less credible, China and the Soviet Union might be more willing to lend political and material support to a North Korean military attack on South Korea. And the Japanese would probably be hesitant to support the Park government economically if U.S. military backing for that government were no longer assured. Once U.S. forces had left, the North Koreans probably reason, the American people would be unlikely to endorse their return in an emergency and

1. For a full exposition of the North Korean position see the memorandum of October 7, 1974, of the Democratic People's Republic of Korea in connection with placing on the agenda of the United Nations General Assembly the item on the withdrawal of all foreign troops in South Korea (U.S. Government, Foreign Broadcast Information Service [FBIS], *Daily Report: East Asia and Pacific,* November 14, 1974, pp. D21–D43), and speech by Foreign Minister Ho Tam on November 8, 1974 (FBIS, *Daily Report: East Asia and Pacific,* November 12, 1974, pp. D1–D14).

2. FBIS, *Daily Report: East Asia and Pacific,* January 28, 1974, p. D1.

3. The North Korean media issue frequent warnings about the alleged aggressive intentions of the Americans and the South Korean authorities, as in the following statement on the fifteenth anniversary of the founding of the Worker-Peasant Red Guards: "Our people are confronted with the urgent task to further increase the defense capacity of the country so as to defend the socialist fatherland and the gains of the revolution as firm as a rock in the face of the ever more undisguised maneuvers of the U.S. imperialists and the Pak Chong-hui clique to provoke a new war" (FBIS, *Daily Report: East Asia and Pacific,* January 15, 1974, p. D3). Of course, it is common practice to allege aggressive intent on the part of potential enemies in order to mobilize support for military preparations, but a case can be made that Kim's behavior stems in part at least from a deep sense of insecurity. See Rinn-sup Shinn, "Changing Perspectives in North Korea: Foreign and Reunification Policies," *Problems of Communism,* vol. 22 (January–February 1973), pp. 55–71.

might also be less inclined than in the past to provide economic and military aid. This view was probably reinforced by the outcome in Vietnam. The North Koreans must thus see the withdrawal of U.S. forces from South Korea as improving in a variety of ways their prospects for eventually gaining control over the South, whether by overt invasion or by backing an insurrection.

Even though Kim Il-sung may assign a low probability to actually achieving early withdrawal of U.S. forces, he gains certain advantages from harping on this theme. By contrasting the alleged dependence of Park Chung-hee on foreign military support with his own vociferous maintenance of the principle of *chu ch'e,* or self-reliance, he confirms his image as a true Korean patriot seeking to reunify the nation without foreign interference. At the same time he tends to weaken Park's position as a nationalist leader. His attacks on the presence of U.S. forces strike responsive chords in many countries of the Third World and among left-wing Japanese, thus strengthening the international position of North Korea. Furthermore, he is able to exploit strong anti-Japanese feelings among Koreans by stressing U.S.–Japanese military cooperation and accusing the United States of scheming to bring the "Japanese militarists" back into Korea. American forces in South Korea constitute in several respects a convenient political target for Kim.

Kim Il-sung might be said, therefore, to have the minimum objective of gaining as much political benefit as possible from attacking the presence of U.S. forces in South Korea and the maximum objective of compelling their withdrawal. He pursues his objectives in Korea by a steady outpouring of propaganda in the North, where he has total control of the media, and through far less effective efforts to reach the people of the South. Outside Korea his main effort during the past two years has been concentrated on pressing the United Nations General Assembly to pass a resolution calling for the dissolution of the UN Command and the withdrawal of all foreign troops from South Korea—"an urgent problem which brooks no further delay."[4]

South Korean Attitudes

The South Koreans are at a fundamental disadvantage geographically compared with the North Koreans, which profoundly affects their state of

4. FBIS, *Daily Report: East Asia and Pacific,* November 14, 1974, p. D21.

mind. Pyongyang's allies demonstrated in the Korean War that they would not permit the destruction of the communist buffer state on their borders. Although the United States similarly rescued the Republic of Korea from destruction in 1950, the fact that it lies thousands of miles away from the Korean peninsula inevitably creates doubt that the survival of the ROK will be as important to Americans as the survival of the Democratic People's Republic of Korea will be to the Chinese and the Russians. This basic asymmetry, as the South Koreans see it, endows Kim Il-sung with a greater feeling of security and hence of tactical flexibility than South Korean leaders could ever have.

South Korean insistence that U.S. forces remain springs from this sense of insecurity. The South Koreans point out that the withdrawal of U.S. forces to Guam or Hawaii would place the United States at a strategic disadvantage in relation to China and the USSR. They regard the prospect of the automatic involvement of U.S. forces in a conflict as a strong deterrent to North Korean attack and urge that they be kept in South Korea until a peace structure guaranteed by the major powers has been established.[5] Park portrays the North Koreans as frustrated by the growing strength of South Korea and seeking to unify Korea by force before South Korea becomes too strong.[6] He told the National Assembly that top priority would be given in 1975 to assuring the continued presence of U.S. forces and to modernizing the South Korean armed forces.[7] The South Korean government has frequently sought from the United States statements of its intention to continue to maintain its forces in Korea. In response, President Ford, when he visited South Korea on November 22, 1974, stated in a joint communiqué with President Park that "the United States has no plan to reduce the present level of United States forces in Korea,"[8] and Secretary of Defense Schlesinger, visiting South Korea in August 1975, gave a similar assurance.[9]

Despite the strong urging by South Korean leaders that U.S. forces remain in South Korea at the present level, there are indications that they expect and are prepared to adjust to withdrawals. Public statements to this

5. See editorial in *Tong-A Ilbo,* March 3, 1974; FBIS, *Daily Report: East Asia and Pacific,* March 5, 1974, p. E3.

6. Commencement address to the Korean Military Academy, March 29, 1974; FBIS, *Daily Report: East Asia and Pacific,* April 1, 1974, p. E1.

7. Policy speech, October 1974; FBIS, *Daily Report: East Asia and Pacific,* October 4, 1974, p. E1.

8. FBIS, *Daily Report: East Asia and Pacific,* November 22, 1974, p. E4.

9. *Washington Post,* August 28, 1975.

effect began to appear several years ago shortly after the United States had withdrawn 20,000 troops. The withdrawal had been vigorously resisted by the South Korean government, but was agreed to when the United States made clear its determination to proceed in any case and promised to strengthen South Korean forces in a five-year modernization program. In August 1970, shortly after the announcement of the withdrawal, Vice President Spiro Agnew visited South Korea and was quoted as saying that the United States would withdraw all its forces from that country in five years provided South Korean forces had been sufficiently modernized by then to stand alone.[10] Defense Secretary Melvin A. Laird, visiting Seoul a year later, did not repeat Agnew's prediction of total withdrawal but did say that the United States might pull out more forces as modernization proceeded.[11]

These statements by highly placed American officials, followed by President Nixon's visit to China and the radical shift in U.S. policy it represented, convinced South Korean leaders that it would be unrealistic to count on U.S. forces remaining in South Korea indefinitely. Premier Kim Chong-pil, in a speech on November 15, 1972, warned that in the new multipolar world nations "are mercilessly pursuing their own interest." To survive, South Korea must cultivate the spirit of independence. "Now is no time to survive through dependence on others," Kim declared. "The U.S. troops now stationed in our country will return home sooner or later. This means that we must defend our country through our own strength."[12]

Heavy emphasis on self-reliance and the need to build up the country's own strength has been a continuing theme in statements of South Korean leaders. Shortly before Schlesinger's visit to Seoul in August 1975, Park told an American correspondent[13] that in four to five years South Korea's armed forces would be sufficiently modernized to be able to defend South Korea against a North Korean attack without air, sea, and logistic support by U.S. forces. Park insisted, however, that "at least until the modernization is fully accomplished, it is absolutely necessary for the United States forces in Korea to be kept at their present level." He admitted that U.S. ground forces were not required even in 1975 to meet a North Korean attack, but stressed the importance of their presence as a guarantee that

10. *Washington Post,* August 27, 1970.
11. *Washington Post,* July 15, 1971.
12. FBIS, *Daily Report: East Asia and Pacific,* November 21, 1972, pp. E3–E4.
13. Interview with Richard Halloran, *New York Times,* August 21, 1975.

the United States would respond to an attack with sea and air forces and as a deterrent to Chinese and Soviet intervention.

In short, the South Korean government would prefer that U.S. forces remain and not be reduced from present levels, but recognizes that the ultimate decision is beyond its control. This is one matter on which the government and the opposition agree, unlike the situation in Thailand, where opposition figures advocated the withdrawal of U.S. forces for several years before the Thai government itself came around to this view. The South Koreans probably genuinely fear that the total withdrawal of U.S. forces would increase the danger of attack by the unpredictable Kim Il-sung and would cause Peking and Moscow to perceive less risk in backing him. American compliance with North Korea's insistent demands would inevitably be seen by many as a victory for North Korea and a defeat for South Korea. Consequently, the South Koreans will employ all the leverage they have to delay a total withdrawal of U.S. forces. They will argue strenuously against any premature reduction of U.S. force levels; if withdrawals cannot be prevented, they will seek from the United States a substantial amount of additional military aid as compensation.

North-South Relations and U.S. Forces

The presence of U.S. forces in South Korea affects several critical determinants of the relationship between the two Koreas: the North-South dialogue, the indigenous force balance, and the rivalry between Seoul and Pyongyang for international recognition and support. It raises questions such as the following: does the presence of U.S. forces strengthen the South Korean government in its negotiations with North Korea, as has been asserted by U.S. spokesmen?[14] Does their presence influence in any way the efforts of South Korea to become as militarily self-sufficient as possible? How does their presence affect the competition for international backing between the two Koreas?

14. For example, by Secretary Schlesinger (*Department of Defense Appropriations for 1975*, Hearings before the Subcommittee on Department of Defense of the House Committee on Appropriations, 93:2, pt. 1 [GPO, 1974], p. 581), and by the Department of State (*Our Commitments in Asia*, Hearings before the Subcommittee on East Asian and Pacific Affairs of the House Committee on Foreign Affairs, 93:2 [GPO, 1974], p. 183).

North-South Dialogue

The North-South dialogue consists of two sets of talks: one between representatives of the Red Cross societies begun in August 1971 and aimed at reuniting families separated by the division of Korea; the other between representatives of the two governments in a North-South coordinating committee established to implement the principles of unification agreed on by high officials of the two governments and jointly announced on July 4, 1972.[15]

Neither series of talks has made perceptible progress. In the Red Cross talks South Korea has called for practical steps to locate aged parents separated from their children and put them in touch with one another, while North Korea has insisted that the first step be the repeal of anti-communist legislation and the disbandment of anticommunist organizations in South Korea. In the North-South coordinating committee talks the South Koreans have maintained that the process of establishing confidence between the two sides should begin with small steps such as cultural exchanges or combining athletes from North and South into a single Korean team at international sports events. The North Koreans have taken the opposite approach, contending that the committee should tackle the really important problems first, and have called for cutting military forces on both sides to 100,000, halting the inflow of weapons from outside Korea, and withdrawing U.S. forces from South Korea. In both sets of talks the North Koreans have held that the presence of American forces in South Korea is the main obstacle to unification. Stalemated by these diametrically opposed views, the talks have deteriorated into formalistic statements, reciprocal charges of bad faith, and bickering over the place of meetings and the membership of delegations. No full-dress meeting of either series has taken place since the summer of 1973, although working-level sessions have continued.

The positions taken in the North-South dialogue reflect the sharply differing official views on Korean unification. South Korea has publicly

15. These principles stipulated that unification should be achieved by Koreans without outside interference; that it should be accomplished by peaceful means; that neither side would defame the other or engage in armed provocation; that exchanges would be carried out in many fields; that both would cooperate positively in the Red Cross talks; that a "hot line" would be installed between Seoul and Pyongyang; and that a North-South coordinating committee would be established to solve various problems between the two sides and settle the unification problem on the basis of the principles agreed on.

taken the position that the division of Korea will probably continue for a long time. Hence, South Koreans argue, it is necessary to adapt to the realities of the changing international situation and through a strategy of "total diplomacy" outdistance North Korea in the competition for international position. Only when South Korea wins both the diplomatic and economic competition will North Korea "show sincerity" in dialogue. Moreover, this international competition will, the South Koreans hope, force North Korea out of isolation and open its society to outside influences, so that in time its internal structure will change.[16]

In contrast to South Korea's characterization of unification as a long-term goal, North Korea calls it "an urgent task which brooks not even a moment's delay."[17] Pyongyang has not only rejected Seoul's gradualist approach, it has increasingly disparaged talks with the present South Korean authorities as a vehicle for achieving unification. For example, in November 1974 North Korean Foreign Minister Ho Tam declared that Park Chung-hee, by calling for the entry of both Koreas into the United Nations, had "unilaterally ruptured the North-South dialogue." Ho went on to say that it was impossible to solve the question of unification through negotiations with the present South Korean authorities, but that the South Korean people had now risen against their rulers and if Park were compelled to step down and a "new democratic figure" came to power, the North-South negotiations could be resumed and the reunification question smoothly resolved.[18] In February 1975 O Chin-u, chief of the general staff of the Korean People's Army, expressed a similar view: "Only by driving out the U.S. imperialist aggressors from South Korea, breaking the Japanese militarists' talons of reinvasion and overthrowing the Pak Chong-hui puppet clique can the South Korean people be freed from their present misfortunes and sufferings and the country's independent peaceful reunification achieved."[19]

16. Kim Chong-pil's news conference, June 23, 1973 (FBIS, *Daily Report: East Asia and Pacific,* June 26, 1973, pp. E1–E7); and Park Chung-hee, *Special Statement Regarding Foreign Policy for Peace and Unification (A Special Commentary)* (Seoul: Korea Information Service, June 1973).

17. Speech by Foreign Minister Ho Tam at a meeting of the Central Committee of the Democratic Front for the Reunification of the Fatherland, November 8, 1974 (FBIS, *Daily Report: East Asia and Pacific,* November 12, 1974, pp. D1–D14).

18. Ibid.

19. Speech on the twenty-seventh anniversary of the Korean People's Army, February 7, 1975 (FBIS, *Daily Report: East Asia and Pacific,* February 11, 1975, p. D12).

So far the only genuine negotiation in the North-South dialogue is the one that produced agreement on setting up the two series of talks, on the statement of the principles of unification, and on the format, time, and place of meetings. In neither series has there been a serious effort to seek out common ground and to narrow differences. Each side seems principally concerned with demonstrating the reasonableness of its own approach to unification and highlighting the intransigence of its opponent. South Korea uses the talks to show interest in unification while gaining time to strengthen its position; North Korea also uses them to show its interest in unification while trying to stimulate domestic opposition to the South Korean government. After three years of sterile confrontation the talks are unlikely to be valued by either government as a vehicle for active promotion of its interests, but neither seems inclined to accept the onus of breaking them off. As long as the talks exist, it is conceivable that both sides will eventually see that their interests lie in agreeing to some form of interaction between their peoples, as East and West Germany have, but the experience of the past three years does not encourage hope that this will happen soon.

If the presence of U.S. forces in South Korea had any effect on this static dialogue, it is difficult to perceive. The withdrawal of a substantial number of U.S. troops in 1971 together with indications that total withdrawal might not be long delayed may have helped persuade North and South Korea—for different reasons—that the time had come to open direct communication with each other. But other considerations were probably more important to the decision to begin talks: the spectacular change in U.S. relations with Peking, the failure of Kim Il-sung's paramilitary intrusions into South Korea in the late 1960s, and Park Chung-hee's concern about growing demands from the opposition for political actions to ease the problems of divided Korea.

Now that the dialogue has been opened, how might it be affected by further withdrawals of U.S. forces? Partial withdrawal might lead Pyongyang to redouble its efforts to bring about total withdrawal; perhaps the collapse of the U.S.-supported governments in Cambodia and South Vietnam and opposition in the United States to Park Chung-hee's domestic policies will encourage it to believe that withdrawal of U.S. forces from South Korea is an irreversible process, as it proved to be in South Vietnam, which could be completed within a few years. Certainly, no partial withdrawal can be expected to make Kim Il-sung drop his demand for total withdrawal. But whether he will continue to insist on fundamental changes or will see advantages in agreeing to small steps will depend more on his appraisal of the stability and longevity of the South Korean government than on decisions by the United States concerning its forces. Hence the problem is to judge not the direct effect of U.S. withdrawals on positions taken by the two sides in the talks, which would probably be slight, but their effect on the stability of the government of South Korea.

Domestic Politics in South Korea

The political strife in South Korea during the past three years, although not directly related to the presence of U.S. forces, raises issues that must be taken into account in reaching decisions on the future of these forces. The quarrel between President Park Chung-hee and his political opposition has encouraged North Koreans to hope that a revolutionary situation is developing in South Korea and has raised doubts among Americans about the future stability of that country, causing some to question the advisability of continuing to maintain U.S. forces there.

Park declared martial law in October 1972, not long after the beginning of the dialogue with North Korea. He then dissolved the National Assembly and introduced a new constitution, which broadened the president's powers considerably and make it possible for him to remain in office indefinitely. These actions were rationalized on the ground that a greater concentration of power was needed in South Korea. Martial law was lifted only after the constitution had been approved by a national referendum carried out under conditions that stifled any organized opposition. A new National Assembly, partly elected, partly appointed by Park, was firmly under his control.

Widespread student demonstrations against Park's actions, stimulated in part by the abduction of opposition leader Kim Tae-chung from a Tokyo hotel to detention in South Korea, broke out in the fall of 1973. These were met by harsh government decrees aimed at suppressing opposition to the new constitution. Resistance soon spread beyond the students to involve Christian leaders, newspapers, and opposition politicians. A series of government actions—including arrests, trials, executions, releases from prison, censoring of the press, the abrogation of some decrees and the adoption of others—failed to subdue the opposition, but the government's determination to maintain the new constitution remained firm.

Altogether, 203 persons were tried under the emergency measures; 8 of them were executed and 28 were still in prison as of June 1975.[20]

After the collapse of the South Vietnamese government in April 1975, Park issued a broad new emergency measure prohibiting political activity by students and advocacy of constitutional revision. It also severely restricted press coverage of certain major domestic political issues. Under the antislander law, in effect since March 1975, Koreans could be prosecuted for criticizing the government or the constitution to foreigners, either in Korea or abroad. Opposition activity lessened during the summer of 1975, owing in part to an increased sense of threat from the North and the consequent greater need for unity in the South felt by South Koreans generally in the wake of the Vietnam debacle and Kim Il-sung's trip to Peking, but the situation remained volatile.

Park's efforts to suppress the opposition and strengthen his hold on power, reported in detail in the American press, evoked strong criticism in this country.[21] In 1974 and 1975 Congress held hearings at which witnesses, including members of Congress, deplored the denial of civil rights to the opponents of the South Korean government.[22] They expressed concern that the U.S. government, through its troop presence in South Korea and its military and economic aid to the South Korean government, was becoming identified with a repressive regime. Some advocated vigorous official action to compel Park to moderate his policies, even by threatening to withhold economic or military aid. To demonstrate congressional concern over this issue, the Foreign Aid Authorization Act for 1974 limited military assistance to South Korea to $145 million unless the President of the United States reported that South Korea had made substantial progress in the observance of human rights, in which case the amount could be increased to $165 million. The administration has also made known to the

20. "Status of Human Rights in the Philippines and South Korea," statement by Assistant Secretary of State Philip C. Habib before the Subcommittee on International Organizations of the House Committee on International Relations, 94:1 (GPO, 1975), pp. 310–13.

21. See, for example, Edwin O. Reischauer and Gregory Henderson, "There's Danger in Korea Still," *New York Times Magazine,* May 20, 1973.

22. *Human Rights in South Korea: Implications for U.S. Policy,* Hearings before the Subcommittees on Asian and Pacific Affairs and on International Organizations and Movements of the House Foreign Affairs Committee, 93:2 (GPO, 1974); *Human Rights in South Korea and the Philippines: Implications for U.S. Policy,* Hearings before the Subcommittee on International Organizations of the House Committee on International Relations, 94:1 (GPO, 1975).

Korean government, both publicly and privately, its disapproval of the denial of human rights in South Korea.[23]

Should repression and resistance intensify in South Korea, opposition among Americans to keeping U.S. forces there would swell. It would be difficult for the U.S. government to justify its close association with an increasingly repressive regime. Support for the Park government in Japan would also decline. Moreover, if Park's measures should greatly widen the circle of opponents and correspondingly narrow his own political base, the danger of a coup or other internal threat to his control would grow. Only the military in South Korea has the power to mount a successful coup and Park's replacement by another military leader would not necessarily improve the outlook for democracy and respect for human rights. It could lead to greater political instability and slower economic growth than has prevailed during the past decade. Political turbulence in South Korea might tempt Kim Il-sung to intervene in ways short of large-scale invasion, creating a confused situation in which it could be difficult for U.S. forces either to intervene or to remain aloof.

Such a grave deterioration of political stability in South Korea seems unlikely, however, at least within the next several years, for awareness of the threat from the North is a great unifier and reduces tendencies toward domestic conflict. Koreans are more accustomed to and tolerant of authoritarian governmental measures than Americans, and Kim Il-sung's intemperate behavior strengthens Park's hand. South Koreans generally agree on the need to be well prepared to defend against North Korean attack and on the desirability of retaining U.S. forces in South Korea for the time being as a deterrent to such an attack. Still, the possibility of continued and intensified political strife within South Korea is real enough that it should be a consideration in deciding the future of the U.S. force presence.

It is not easy to judge the effect of the U.S. forces on domestic politics in South Korea. Their presence has not prevented the South Korean government from curtailing political freedom during the past several years, but repression might have been more severe had it not been for that government's desire to keep American forces there and to continue to receive other forms of U.S. support. In a very general way the forces may contribute to stability in South Korea by diminishing the fear of war, but for the most part political stability—or the lack of it—is determined by the play of internal forces.

---

23. Habib, "Status of Human Rights in the Philippines and South Korea."

The U.S. government could, if it chose to do so, undermine Park's position by threatening to withdraw its forces and intimating that U.S. support for South Korea was uncertain so long as Park remained in power. On the other hand, the withdrawal of U.S. forces in a few years by agreement with Park, after modernization of South Korean forces had been completed, might strengthen rather than weaken his position if the South Koreans closed ranks in recognition of the need to assume greater responsibility for their own defense. But a threat to withdraw U.S. forces is a blunt instrument. There is little assurance that its use would lead either to greater democracy and political freedom in South Korea or to greater political stability there, and it could easily increase the danger of conflict, the prevention of which is a primary purpose of U.S. policy.

The Drive for Military Self-Sufficiency

The South Korean government is working hard to raise its forces, through modernization, to a level at which it could face the North Korean military threat with confidence even though U.S. forces were no longer in South Korea. To this end the National Assembly in July 1975 enacted a national defense tax aimed at raising an additional $400 million annually over the next five years. The Republic of Korea has also rapidly increased its cash purchases of military equipment from the United States. These amounted to $1.3 million in fiscal 1973, $56.4 million in fiscal 1974, and $159.8 million in fiscal 1975. In the latter year cash purchases exceeded the value of U.S. military aid to South Korea.[24] The South Korean government was reliably reported to be shopping also for substantial amounts of military equipment in Europe.

The "military self-sufficiency" that this program aims at attaining in four to five years is not an ability to produce all the military equipment and supplies required to maintain a modern force or to fight a sustained conflict. South Korea would still have to purchase modern weapons from the United States or elsewhere to prevent a military imbalance with North Korea from developing, and in the event of conflict South Korean forces would still need early replacement and resupply from outside. The Republic of Korea would continue to rely on the U.S. defense commitment as a deterrent to intervention by Chinese or Soviet military forces. Moreover, the expansion of the South Korean economy along lines now envisioned by the government will make the country increasingly dependent

24. See table 2–2.

on foreign trade and foreign investment. Thus the "military self-sufficiency" sought by South Korea is a rather narrowly defined self-sufficiency, meaning a capability to defend against North Korean attack without intervention by U.S. forces but with a continuing flow of U.S. supplies and equipment and U.S. willingness to hold the line against intervention by a big power.

One aspect of South Korea's drive for military self-sufficiency—the nuclear option—deserves special attention. Although the Republic of Korea signed and ratified the nuclear nonproliferation treaty (NPT) and publicly disavowed any intention to develop nuclear weapons, President Park Chung-hee has declared that the country would develop them if the United States withdrew its nuclear umbrella. But he quickly added that he considered this unlikely.[25] Secretary Schlesinger told Congress in March 1975 that the withdrawal of U.S. forces from Northeast Asia (presumably including Japan as well as South Korea) would lead South Korea to build nuclear weapons.

South Korea might be capable of producing and testing a nuclear weapon as early as the late 1980s should its leaders decide to make the large investment required and suffer the international consequences, especially the damage to relations with the United States and Japan. It has many scientists and engineers, and its Atomic Energy Research Institute has carried on research in nuclear science since obtaining its first experimental nuclear reactor in 1962. It has an ambitious nuclear power program: its first nuclear power station, equipped with American "light water" nuclear reactors, is now under construction and scheduled for completion in 1976, and five more are planned. It is also making arrangements to purchase from Canada a "heavy water" nuclear reactor similar to the one from which India obtained the materials for its nuclear explosion.[26]

South Korea's nuclear reactors are all, of course, subject to inspection under a safeguards agreement with the International Atomic Energy Agency, and Canada is negotiating a special safeguards agreement with South Korea intended to close the loopholes that existed in the Canadian agreement with India. Consequently, there are important political as well as technological obstacles to South Korea's acquiring the grade of fissionable material necessary to manufacture nuclear weapons. Nevertheless, such is the overlap in the scientific and engineering skills required for peaceful and weapon uses of nuclear energy that the South Koreans could,

25. *Washington Post,* June 27, 1975.
26. *Washington Post,* June 28, 1975.

without violating their international commitments, take all the preliminary steps in a nuclear weapon program short of putting together the weapon itself. They have already entered into negotiations with a French firm for the purchase of a small, laboratory-size reprocessing plant to separate plutonium from the spent fuel of nuclear reactors. They might also attempt to acquire a small centrifuge system for enriching natural uranium. Like the reprocessing plant, an enrichment facility could be justified as meeting the future needs of South Korea's nuclear power program, although it would be technically difficult to construct and operate and almost certainly would require some cooperation from an advanced country. But the South Koreans might well consider such preparations a prudent hedge against the possible withdrawal of U.S. protection.

Some members of Congress have expressed concern about the possibility that South Korea might develop nuclear weapons. Representative Les Aspin even demanded that the shipment of enriched uranium from the United States to fuel South Korea's power reactors be halted, asserting that the plutonium by-product of uranium scheduled to be shipped during 1975–76 would be sufficient to produce one hundred atomic bombs,[27] although to obtain plutonium for making weapons, South Korea not only would have to acquire a reprocessing plant large enough to process this quantity of spent fuel, but would have to withdraw from the NPT. Using spent fuel to produce nuclear weapons would obviously jeopardize the continued access to the U.S. enriched uranium needed to keep South Korea's nuclear power industry in operation.

A decision by the United States to withdraw its forces from Korea would increase South Korean compulsion to become more self-sufficient militarily, but it is unlikely that the pace of the drive now under way could be much accelerated. South Korea would also feel greater need to develop the skills and facilities required to produce nuclear weapons, although it probably would not actually manufacture and test them unless its confidence in and dependence on the United States had greatly declined.

The Rivalry for International Position

Since the beginning of the North-South dialogue, rivalry between the two Korean governments for international recognition and support has intensified. Many governments that once had diplomatic relations with South Korea have now established relations with North Korea as well. The

27. *New York Times*, April 24, 1975.

United Nations has also become an important arena for North-South contention. In a surprise reversal of its long-held position, South Korea proposed in June 1973 that both Koreas be admitted to the United Nations, as a provisional arrangement pending unification. North Korea, however, denounced the proposal as a device to perpetuate division, and it has not attracted the international support that Seoul hoped for. Consequently, for some time to come both governments are likely to be present at the United Nations in observer status only.

For the past two years the North Koreans have urged the United Nations General Assembly to pass a resolution calling for the dissolution of the UN Command in Korea and the withdrawal of U.S. forces. By informal arrangements between the opposing sides, the resolution was not put to the vote in the 1973 session of the General Assembly. The following year, however, a similar resolution was brought to a vote in the Political Committee of the General Assembly. Despite the earlier passage by a substantial majority of a U.S.-sponsored resolution referring to the Security Council the question of dissolving the UN Command and new arrangements to maintain the essential elements of the armistice, the resolution backed by North Korea, China, and the Soviet Union was barely defeated in a tie vote, 48–48 with 38 abstentions. Pressure clearly was growing to eliminate the UN Command, which a large number of UN members regarded as an outmoded holdover from the early days of the cold war.

In June 1975 the United States informed the Security Council that it was ready, in consultation with the government of the Republic of Korea, to terminate the UN Command by January 1, 1976, and to designate military officers of the United States and the Republic of Korea as successors in command, provided the Korean People's Army and the Chinese People's Volunteers, as signatories to the armistice agreement, affirmed that the agreement would continue in force. At the same time the United States, joined by other countries, submitted to the General Assembly a draft resolution expressing hope that the Security Council would encourage the parties directly concerned to undertake discussions leading to the dissolution of the UN Command together with appropriate arrangements to maintain the armistice agreement. Subsequently, North Korean supporters in the United Nations submitted a rival resolution to the General Assembly that called for the dissolution of the UN Command and the withdrawal of all foreign forces from South Korea. Both resolutions, despite their contradictory recommendations, were passed by the General Assembly in November 1975. The General Assembly, however, could not dissolve the UN Command by its action alone; only the Security Council has that power.

Since the United States and South Korea have indicated that they intend to keep U.S. forces in South Korea by bilateral agreement, even if the UN eventually dissolved the UN Command these forces would not be affected. There is still the question, however, of the effect the continued presence of U.S. forces there may have on the international prestige and position of the Republic of Korea in its competition with the Democratic People's Republic of Korea. North Korean propaganda has stressed the principle of self-reliance, has insisted on the unification of Korea by Koreans without foreign interference, and has denounced the U.S. military presence in Korea as the main obstacle to reunification. In an atmosphere of growing polarization over various issues between the Third World and the developed states, the close association between the United States and the Republic of Korea symbolized by the presence of U.S. forces on South Korean soil may significantly handicap the ROK's efforts to gain broad international support for its position. It may help to explain why the August 1975 conference of nonaligned nations in Lima, Peru, accepted North Korea as one of their number, despite its security treaties with both China and the USSR, but rejected South Korea.

South Korea has expressed willingness to develop relations with "nonhostile" communist countries and has made various overtures to the Soviet Union and China. The USSR initially responded cautiously but positively by admitting a few South Koreans to international meetings in Moscow. Pyongyang's strong adverse reaction and Moscow's fear of losing ground to Peking appear to have caused the Russians to back away, although they acknowledge privately that a "German formula" would produce a more stable Korea. So far as is known, the Chinese have not responded favorably to South Korean probes or been willing to entertain, even privately, the idea of applying the German formula to Korea.

North Korea, while adamantly opposing any contact whatsoever between its allies and South Korea, already trades and has other forms of interchange with Japan. It has also admitted a few Americans on visits and has proposed negotiating a peace treaty with the United States. Kim Il-sung is working vigorously to gain a stronger international position than South Korea's, especially with the four big powers most concerned with Korea.

Neither the United States nor Japan is in a position to control the contacts of its nationals with North Korea to the extent that China and the

Soviet Union can control the contacts of theirs with South Korea. North Korea has shown that it can exert more effective pressure on its allies on this issue than can South Korea on the United States or Japan. The presence of U.S. forces in South Korea can be viewed in a political sense as helping to counterbalance these North Korean advantages by providing palpable assurance to the South Korean government and people that their ties with the United States remain strong. These ties are far more important to South Korea than support from Third World states. The withdrawal of U.S. forces would weaken the ties and represent a setback for South Korea in the contest for international position.

CHAPTER FOUR

THE POLITICAL SIGNIFICANCE OF
U.S. FORCES: THE BIG POWERS

The attitudes of the Soviet Union, China, and Japan toward the presence of U.S. forces in South Korea are more complicated than those of the two Korean governments. The big powers are naturally less concerned with what happens in Korea than with the impact on their overall national interests of what may happen there. The Chinese and Soviet positions on U.S. forces in South Korea are strongly affected by the Sino-Soviet dispute and by concern for their bilateral relations with the United States and Japan. The Japanese view these forces primarily in relation to the U.S. security commitment to Japan.

Soviet Views

The USSR has a security interest in preventing an unfriendly major power from gaining predominant influence in neighboring Korea. Consequently, before withdrawing its occupation forces after World War II, it established a client government in the northern part of the divided country and became its chief supplier of economic and military aid. With the outbreak of the Sino-Soviet dispute, however, the People's Republic of China became an overt rival for influence in Pyongyang and an important provider of aid. Rivalry between the two communist powers has made it possible for North Korea to play one off against the other and thus gain considerable freedom of action.

The current attitude of the Soviet Union toward Korea is governed less by concern for its bilateral relations with North Korea than by its policies toward the other three big powers with interests in Korea: the United States, Japan, and China. To avoid losing influence relative to China, it will respond somewhat to North Korean pressure, but not to the point of seriously interfering with its more important objectives of maintaining détente with the United States and improving relations with Japan. The small amount of space devoted to relations with Korea by Soviet media in the past several years indicates that they are not a high-priority issue for Moscow, perhaps because relative stability has prevailed on the Korean peninsula. For example, the Russians have not provided the North Koreans with some of the advanced weapons they have given to certain Arab states. Policies toward Korea followed by the Soviet Union in recent years suggest that it strongly favors continued stability there and the avoidance of renewed conflict, which would endanger the achievement of its broader global aims.

Moscow from time to time calls for the withdrawal of U.S. forces from Korea but shows little zeal in thus backing its North Korean ally. Soviet media have not treated withdrawal as a major issue. Most statements on the subject appear on ceremonial occasions, such as the anniversary of the founding of the Democratic People's Republic of Korea, the signing of the mutual defense treaty with Pyongyang, or the annual "month of solidarity with the people of the DPRK." They are mildly worded, even in broadcasts in Korean to Korea, in sharp contrast to Pyongyang's lurid invective. Moreover, the Russians do not, as the North Koreans frequently do, charge that U.S. forces in South Korea are there in pursuance of aggressive American schemes for war on the socialist states, for bringing the "Japanese militarists" back into Korea, or for preparing an attack on North Korea. In fact, Soviet statements frequently do not identify these forces as American but simply refer to them as "foreign troops."[1] The Soviet Union has firmly supported the resolutions considered by the United Nations General Assembly calling for the withdrawal of foreign troops stationed in Korea under the UN flag. But the Soviet Union has not undertaken any initiative of its own on the issue.

Although the USSR endorses the principle of Korean reunification and North Korean proposals to that end, its behavior strongly suggests that it

1. Examples of Soviet commentary on Korea can be found in U.S. Government, Foreign Broadcast Information Service (FBIS), *Daily Report: Soviet Union*: article by A. Malyshkin in *Krasnaya Zvezda*, July 27, 1972 (*Daily Report*, August 3, 1972, pp. C1, C2); article by Y. Shtykanov in *Izvestiya*, September 8, 1972 (*Daily Report*, September 12, 1972, pp. C6, C7); commentary by Ligonov (in Korean to Korea), April 7, 1973 (*Daily Report*, April 10, 1973, pp. C4, C5); commentary by Nikolayev (in Korean to Korea), June 20, 1973 (*Daily Report*, July 6, 1973, pp. C1, C2); commentary by Nikolayev (in Korean to Korea), August 23, 1974 (*Daily Report*, September 4, 1974, pp. M2, M3); article by Col. M. Ponomarev and A. Malyshkin in *Krasnaya Zvezda*, December 15, 1974 (*Daily Report*, December 31, 1974, p. M1).

sees little prospect that Korea will be reunited within the next few years and would rather live with a divided Korea than undergo the costs and risks of backing a renewed attempt by Kim Il-sung to unite the peninsula by force. Private comments by Soviet officials and scholars also indicate that Moscow sees long-term coexistence of the two Koreas as probable and therefore tends to favor practical steps to reduce tension and the risk of war, comparable to those taken by East and West Germany.[2]

The Soviet preference for stability in Korea helps explain why Moscow has not made a big issue of the presence of U.S. forces in South Korea. And were the Russians to press hard for withdrawal, they would engender increased suspicion and antagonism among Americans and Japanese, which would hinder their efforts to fortify détente and to expand economic relations with the United States and Japan. The statements they have made are probably considered the minimum necessary to avoid suffering loss of influence in Pyongyang relative to China.

There is little evidence that the Soviet Union considers U.S. forces in South Korea a significant threat to their interests under present circumstances. Indeed, they may well view them as a useful brake on reckless action by Kim Il-sung that could bring the USSR into dangerous confrontation with the United States. Conflict in Korea would create a fluid and perhaps rapidly changing situation in which the Chinese might gain an opportunity to expand their influence in Pyongyang at Moscow's expense. And the Japanese might be impelled to increase their military power substantially. For all these reasons, Moscow seems likely to be tolerant of a continued U.S. military presence in Korea. The Russians will probably continue to work in the United Nations for the dissolution of the UN Command, although they would not expect the passage of a resolution to this effect to bring about the withdrawal of U.S. forces.

2. A revealing commentary broadcast in Korean to Korea not long after the July 1972 agreement on the principles of unification warmly welcomed the opening of the dialogue between North Korea and South Korea and contained the remarkably balanced statement that "both sides have many problems to solve if they want to remove the old obstacles in order to bring the two sides together. This can only be done if the two parties take realistic attitudes and show goodwill. There is an old Korean saying that a distance of 1000 ri [Korean unit of distance] begins with one step." The commentary added that "the general atmosphere of detente on the international scene provides favorable conditions for the talks between South and North Korea" and referred approvingly to the precedent of East and West Germany. Commentary by Ligonov, November 20, 1972; FBIS, *Daily Report: Soviet Union,* November 22, 1972, pp. C2, C3.

Chinese Views

China has an even stronger security interest than the USSR in preventing the domination of Korea by an unfriendly power, for it not only has a much longer border with Korea than the Soviet Union has, but that border is close to China's industrial heartland. During the first half of this century, the Chinese saw the Japanese develop Korea into a base from which they occupied Manchuria and then proceeded to invade the rest of China. The recent memory of this invasion from Korea was doubtless critical in persuading Chinese leaders in 1950 that despite their military weakness they must at all costs prevent the establishment of hostile power along the Yalu River.

In the competition with the Soviet Union for influence on the independent-minded Kim Il-sung, China has certain advantages, including deep-rooted cultural and racial affinities and common membership in the Third World, which, on many issues, aligns them with North Korea against the superpowers and Japan. Since Chou En-lai's visit to Pyongyang in April 1970 to repair the damage Sino-Korean relations had suffered during the Cultural Revolution, the two governments have been close. But China cannot compete with the USSR in providing advanced military and industrial equipment. This Soviet advantage, together with Kim's strong determination to keep North Korea as self-reliant and independent as possible, prevents Chinese domination and preserves Pyongang's freedom of maneuver.

China, like the USSR, gives priority to its relations with the United States and Japan over its relations with North Korea. China's rapprochement with the United States, which clearly came as a shock to North Korea, and its subsequent normalization of relations with Japan made the Chinese less vigorous in their support of North Korea. They have toned down their attacks on U.S. policy toward Korea and have dropped the accusation that the United States is scheming to bring the Japanese militarists back into Korea. A wide gap has appeared between the strident North Korean attacks on the United States and Japan and the relatively moderate tone of the Chinese.[3] The Chinese have, however, sought to miti-

3. Compare, for example, the speeches given at Peking banquets by Chief of General Staff Huang Yung-sheng in 1971 (FBIS, *Daily Report: People's Republic of China,* September 7, 1971, pp. A11–A13) and Politburo member Chen Hsi-lien in

gate North Korean unhappiness with the Chinese move to cultivate better relations with the United States and Japan. For example, in September 1971, shortly after the announcement of President Nixon's intention to visit China, they signed a new military aid agreement with North Korea.

Before 1974 Chinese demands for the withdrawal of U.S. forces from Korea were infrequent and almost invariably consisted of a standard formula proclaimed, like the Soviet Union's, on a special occasion, such as the anniversary of the entry of the Chinese People's Volunteers into the war in Korea, or in connection with the debate on Korea in the United Nations. In private conversations with foreign diplomats the Chinese occasionally gave the impression that the continued presence of U.S. forces in South Korea did not particularly disturb them. In the fall of 1973 Chinese diplomats in New York cooperated in working out a compromise solution that, in effect, postponed confrontation over the UN Command issue. Since that time, however, they have taken a harder line. They showed no disposition to compromise on the UN Command issue in the fall of 1974; UN representative Huang Hua's attacks on the presence of U.S. forces in South Korea in November were harsher than those of the Soviet representative and frequently criticized the forces by name rather than under the Soviet-preferred euphemism of "foreign forces." The Chinese now seem disinclined, even in private, to depart from the official public position that U.S. forces should be withdrawn from South Korea. Furthermore, when Kim Il-sung visited Peking in April 1975, China for the first time publicly recognized North Korea as "the sole legal sovereign state of the Korean

---

1974 (FBIS, *Daily Report: People's Republic of China,* October 25, 1974, p. A8). Huang referred to "our common enemies, U.S. imperialism and Japanese militarism," and pledged "to fight shoulder to shoulder with the Korean people and army in our common cause of opposing the U.S. aggressors and all their running dogs." Chen made no reference to "U.S. imperialism," "Japanese militarism," or "U.S. aggressors." He called on the United States to "stop interfering in Korea's internal affairs immediately" and to pull its troops flying the UN flag out of South Korea "without delay." He added that "the government and people of China have always given resolute support to the Korean people in their just struggle for the independent and peaceful reunification of their country." Meanwhile, the North Koreans continue to broadcast accusations such as the following: "the U.S. imperialist war-maniacs are bringing into bolder relief their wild design for Asian aggression . . . by more zealously putting up the Japanese militarists as 'shock forces' of aggression" (FBIS, *Daily Report: East Asia and Pacific,* March 5, 1975, p. D1). Note also the restraint of Teng Hsiao-p'ing in his speech of April 18, 1975, at a Peking banquet, in contrast to Kim Il-sung's threats at the same banquet (FBIS, *Daily Report: People's Republic of China,* April 21, 1975, pp. A7–A18).

nation,"[4] although apparently it did not encourage military action by North Korea against South Korea.[5]

The Chinese periodically come out with statements supporting the "independent and peaceful reunification" of Korea. The repeated references to "peaceful" reunification emphasize China's unwillingness to back renewed resort to force. Although Kim Il-sung uses the same phrase, he surrounds it with belligerent rhetoric suggesting that North Korea is much more willing to use force. Chinese description of the projected reunification as "independent," while implying that withdrawal of U.S. forces is a prime requisite, also implies that China does not wish to be involved in bringing it about. Unlike the Russians, the Chinese do not acknowledge in private conversations that Korea is likely to remain divided for a long time. Yet there is little evidence, in either China's behavior or its public statements, that it expects unification within the foreseeable future. For China, as for the Soviet Union, it is not a high-priority issue.

Although recent Chinese behavior raises some doubt about whether the Chinese continue to regard with equanimity the presence of U.S. forces in South Korea, there are strong reasons to believe that an early withdrawal of U.S. forces would create uncertainty and risk in the years immediately ahead that China, in view of its international position, would prefer to avoid. The Chinese probably recognize, for example, that early withdrawal would increase the risk of conflict in Korea and that such a conflict would gravely undermine China's efforts to strengthen its position relative to the Soviet Union by cultivating its relations with the United States and Japan. Conflict would increase Pyongyang's dependence on the USSR for advanced weapons and could result in the Soviet Union's gaining a stronger position in North Korea at Chinese expense, as appears to have happened in North Vietnam. Also, conflict in Korea would increase the risk of remilitarization of Japan, an outcome that China could hardly view with favor.

The Chinese are patently worried about the strengthening of Soviet military forces in the western Pacific, Soviet efforts to woo the Japanese, and what the Chinese perceive as a scheme to encircle China by drawing its neighbors into a Soviet-sponsored collective security agreement. The Chinese have told the Japanese they regard the U.S.–Japanese security treaty and the Japanese self-defense force as necessary counters to Russian

4. FBIS, *Daily Report: People's Republic of China,* April 28, 1975, p. A17.

5. *New York Times,* May 29, 1975, quoting "State Department officials."

expansionist designs.[6] They do not object to U.S. forces in and around Japan, which add credibility to the U.S. commitment. Withdrawal of U.S. forces from South Korea so soon after their withdrawal from mainland Southeast Asia might easily appear to the Chinese as a prelude to a general U.S. withdrawal from Northeast Asia, which would result in increased Soviet influence in the region.

For all of these reasons it is difficult to believe that the Chinese genuinely desire an early withdrawal of U.S. forces from South Korea. The hardening of their position can probably be explained by North Korea's extreme sensitivity and China's rivalry with the USSR for influence on Pyongyang. The Chinese may well believe that they can take a hard line on this issue, consonant with their strongly voiced opposition to the stationing of forces of the superpowers anywhere outside their own territory, without significantly increasing the possibility that U.S. forces will actually withdraw from South Korea soon. It would be in line with China's long-term aims to have the United Nations formally call for the withdrawal yet not harmful to China's short-term interest in countering the Soviet Union, since the Chinese too are aware that U.S. forces would remain in South Korea even if the United Nations should dissolve the UN Command.

Japanese Views

The attitude of Japan is a crucial factor in decisions about U.S. forces in Korea because of the importance to the United States of its relations with Japan. Indeed, the principal justification for the U.S. defense commitment to South Korea and the presence of U.S. forces there is the potential damage to U.S.–Japanese relations that would result from the military conquest of South Korea by North Korea. But there is no common view of Korea among Japanese—their attitudes are complicated by a history of ill will between Japanese and Koreans and by a deep split over foreign policy between conservatives and leftists in Japan.

Japanese governments have traditionally regarded Korea as important to the security of Japan. Wars with China and Russia around the turn of the century were fought in part for the control of the Korean peninsula,

6. Statements by Chou En-lai to Japanese Liberal Democratic party Diet members Takeo Kimura, January 1973 (*Yomiuri* and *Washington Post,* January 19, 1973) and Shigeru Hori, January 1975 (*Japan Times Weekly* [international edition], February 1, 1975, p. 1).

which became a Japanese colony in 1910 and remained in Japanese hands until 1945. Since World War II, however, although the view that Korea is important to Japan's security persists, especially among conservatives, Japanese governments are less able to influence the situation there than in the past, having renounced both claims to Korean territory and the use of military force except in defense of the homeland. They have relied on the U.S. government to ensure a Korean government in the southern half of the peninsula that is relatively friendly to Japan. The U.S. commitment to South Korea and the presence of U.S. forces there prevent the domination of the peninsula by a major power unfriendly to Japan. At the same time American bases in Japan are vital—or at least very important—to the ability of the United States to intervene militarily in the defense of South Korea. Thus the attitudes of the Japanese toward Korea have become inextricably linked to their attitudes toward the U.S.–Japanese alliance.

Premier Eisaku Sato's statement that the security of South Korea was "essential to Japan's own security" reflected this linkage.[7] The U.S. government wanted a public expression of the Japanese security interest in South Korea to demonstrate to Congress that the reversion of Okinawa to Japan would not impair the ability of the United States to fulfill its security commitment to South Korea. Sato complied, somewhat reluctantly, not only by including the above statement in the communiqué, but also by publicly declaring that the Japanese response to a U.S. request to use military bases in Japan to defend South Korea would be prompt and positive.[8] Sato was reluctant not because he lacked concern for South Korea's security, but because he knew that a public statement of that concern would be widely misinterpreted in Japan and elsewhere as foreshadowing Japanese assumption of military responsibility for South Korea. Subsequent attacks on the statement by the opposition and even by some members of the ruling Liberal Democratic party, while reinforcing the widely shared determination in Japan not to undertake defense responsibilities outside national territory, did not shake the conviction of the Japanese government and its principal supporters that South Korea's security is important to Japan.

The collapse of the South Vietnamese government heightened Japanese anxiety about the security of Japan. While they knew that Americans re-

---

7. Nixon-Sato communiqué, November 21, 1969 (U.S. Department of State, *United States Foreign Policy 1969–1970: A Report of the Secretary of State*, Publication 8575 [1971], pp. 503–05).

8. *Washington Post*, November 22, 1969.

garded Japan as far more important than Vietnam, the Japanese could not ignore the increased power of Congress to limit the President's freedom of action in foreign affairs or Americans' reaction against "excessive" involvement abroad. They have therefore engaged in the most forthright debate on defense issues that has occurred since World War II, with much attention focused on Korea.

For most Japanese Indochina is far away and not closely related to Japan's security, but Korea is next door. Consequently, many of them are asking whether Korea will be the next battleground in Asia and, if so, how the United States will respond.[9] Anxiety about the possible eruption of conflict in Korea was intensified by Kim Il-sung's sudden visit to Peking just after Hanoi's victory in Vietnam. In this changed atmosphere, Japanese leaders have made a series of statements supporting the continued presence of U.S. forces in South Korea.

Even before the Saigon government toppled, Japanese Foreign Minister Kiichi Miyazawa on an official visit to Washington in early April 1975 felt impelled to ask for and received renewed assurance of the U.S. government's commitment to the defense of Japan. On his return to Tokyo Miyazawa repeated before the Diet Sato's statement in the 1969 communiqué.[10] Later, in an interview with an American correspondent, he warned that a sudden withdrawal of U.S. forces from South Korea would be "a shock of such magnitude as to make its effect totally unpredictable."[11] During former Secretary of Defense Schlesinger's visit to Japan in August 1975, he and Michita Sakata, director general of the Japanese Defense Agency, agreed that the presence of U.S. forces in Korea was essential to the stability of the peninsula.[12] Shortly before Schlesinger's visit, Premier Takeo Miki and President Ford had agreed in Washington, in an updated version of the Nixon-Sato statement on Korea, that "the security of the Republic of Korea is essential to the maintenance of peace on the Korean peninsula, which in turn is necessary for the peace and security of East Asia, including Japan."[13] All these reaffirmations of the importance to Japan of the U.S. commitment to South Korea demonstrate

9. *New York Times,* May 14, 1975.

10. *Asahi,* April 16, 1975.

11. Interview with Tom Braden, *Washington Post,* August 2, 1975. Interestingly, Miyazawa said that the reaction to a gradual withdrawal or to the withdrawal of U.S. ground forces only would be different. In such circumstances, he thought, the opposition parties might come to their senses and a "new realism" would reign.

12. *Japan Times Weekly* (international edition), September 6, 1975.

13. *Japan Report,* vol. 1 (September 1, 1975), p. 2.

how closely the Japanese government and people will be watching U.S. actions regarding its forces in South Korea.

Those favoring the presence of U.S. forces in South Korea include the mainstream of the Liberal Democratic party, business leaders, the Foreign Ministry, the Defense Agency, and other important elements of the bureaucracy. For this group, the U.S. military presence serves a number of purposes. By diminishing the risk of conflict, it improves the climate for Japanese trade and investment in South Korea, which have become increasingly important to Japanese business. (South Korea in 1974 was second only to the United States as a market for Japanese exports and was a leading recipient of Japanese government development loans and private investment.) It counters the nearby presence of Soviet and Chinese forces and the corollary influence of these nations in Korea and provides a firm base for the coordination of U.S. and Japanese policies toward South Korea. It eliminates any need for Japan to consider providing forces for the defense of South Korea and makes it more difficult for right-wing elements in Japan to use the threat to South Korea as a justification for stronger Japanese armed forces. Perhaps most important of all, the presence of U.S. forces in South Korea strengthens the credibility of the U.S. commitment to the defense not only of that nation, but, by extension, of Japan itself.

Japanese who oppose the U.S.–Japanese security treaty, principally the Japanese Socialist party and the Japanese Communist party, also oppose the presence of U.S. forces in South Korea. They favor North Korea over South Korea and see no danger to Japan in Kim Il-sung's taking over South Korea. On the contrary, they believe the presence of U.S. forces in South Korea increases the risk that Japan might be dragged into a war by the United States, a risk that they see as being further intensified by the growing Japanese economic stake in South Korea. They argue that Japanese security can best be maintained by severing the defense link with the United States, thus causing the removal of U.S. forces and bases from both Japan and Korea, and relying on a policy of neutrality to protect Japan's interests against China or the Soviet Union or efforts by either of these states to use their influence in Korea to Japan's disadvantage.

There is little prospect that any coalition favoring an end to Japan's security relationship with the United States will come to power in the foreseeable future. The opposition to the Liberal Democratic party is too deeply split into competing parties and factions. But the LDP has been slowly losing ground in national and local elections for some time, and it is conceivable that within a few years it might be forced to form a coalition with one of the smaller parties such as the Democratic Socialist party or the Komeito. In a coalition government, support for U.S.–Japanese security arrangements and for U.S. forces in Korea probably would be weakened.

So long as the LDP government remains in power there is likely to be little change in its support for the presence of U.S. forces in South Korea, for the reasons stated above. The Japanese government will acquiesce in the dissolution of the UN Command, if that becomes unavoidable, but will continue to favor the presence of U.S. forces under the U.S.–South Korean security treaty.

The primary concern of the Japanese government is to prevent renewed conflict in Korea, and it sees U.S. forces as an important deterrent to any aggressive move by Kim Il-sung. The outbreak of war in Korea would set off a bitter controversy in Japan over the use by the United States of bases in Japan to intervene in support of South Korea. Major demonstrations might be mounted to interfere with such use. Politicians opposing the government on this issue would be backed by large numbers of Japanese, motivated by the general Japanese dislike of Koreans, the critical attitude of many intellectuals toward the South Korean government, or just the fear of being involved in war. Although ultimately most Japanese would probably come around to accepting the government's position, controversy over the issue could severely strain relations between the United States and Japan. The Japanese government would therefore be reluctant to see U.S. forces removed from South Korea if this action appeared to increase in any way the risk of conflict there.

CHAPTER FIVE

CHOICES FOR THE UNITED STATES

In considering whether to withdraw any or all of the U.S. forces in South Korea, the critical question is whether the withdrawals would significantly increase the risk that war would break out again between the two Koreas. Such a conflict would not only create turmoil in Japan and place severe strain on U.S.–Japanese relations; it would also force the United States to choose between becoming involved in another war on the Asian mainland and facing the consequences of the probable collapse of Japanese confidence in its security commitment to Japan. Those consequences would be serious. The Japanese might initially take refuge in neutralism and accommodation with their powerful neighbors. But a country as big and important as Japan would almost certainly turn before long to strengthening its own military power, perhaps ultimately acquiring nuclear weapons. A rearmed Japan, no longer closely linked to the United States, would alarm the smaller nations of the region and would compel China and the Soviet Union to strengthen their military forces. U.S. efforts to diminish tension and reduce the danger of war in East Asia would have suffered a severe setback.

Because the consequences of renewed conflict in Korea would be so serious, the United States should avoid taking actions that would weaken the deterrent to a North Korean attack. No U.S. forces should be withdrawn unless there are good grounds for confidence that South Korean forces plus a credible U.S. determination to intervene militarily will continue to deter Kim Il-sung, as they have for over twenty years. Kim's belligerence, the inevitable uncertainty about his intentions, and the difficulty of predicting with assurance the outcome of a conflict make it wiser to overinsure than to underinsure.

There have been some expressions of concern that the South Koreans might start a conflict in the hope of compelling the United States to back

49

them in a march north. Such an attack would make little sense from the viewpoint of South Korea, which has far more to gain from biding its time and building its strength. And uncertainty about the U.S. reaction—especially after Vietnam—and the near certainty that China and the Soviet Union would intervene to prevent the extinction of North Korea virtually rule out a South Korean attempt to unify the nation by force.

The Short-Term Outlook

The fall of Pnom Penh and Saigon has convincingly demonstrated to Southeast Asians that the United States is unlikely to intervene again militarily in their region. South Koreans and Japanese are also questioning whether the United States intends to stand by its defense commitment in Northeast Asia. In this changed atmosphere, even a partial withdrawal of U.S. forces from South Korea within the next year or two would be interpreted by many as the beginning of an American military disengagement from Northeast Asia. It would shake South Korean and Japanese confidence in the determination of the United States to maintain its defense commitment to both countries. No matter how vigorously the United States argued that the withdrawals did not significantly affect the military balance in Korea, it would probably be impossible to blunt the political impact. The action would increase the risk of an attack on South Korea by North Korea and cause many more Japanese than in the past to seriously consider alternatives to reliance on the U.S. security commitment.

This danger appears to be generally recognized in Washington. Pressure in Congress for an early reduction of U.S. forces in both Europe and Northeast Asia has slackened. It seems widely accepted that time is needed to evaluate the effect of developments in Indochina on the global position of the United States before deciding whether it is advisable to further weaken the U.S. military position overseas. The U.S. government has declared that it intends to maintain its forces in South Korea whatever action may be taken by the United Nations regarding the UN Command.

A Medium-Term Plan

Two years or more from now, when the early after-effects of the collapse in Vietnam have been absorbed, it will be possible to consider the question of U.S. forces in South Korea on its own merits in the light of circumstances at that time, with less risk that a decision to withdraw some would appear to be an isolationist reaction to the defeat of American policy in Vietnam.

It could be argued that the most prudent course for the United States would be to adhere indefinitely to its reliance on roughly the present U.S. force deployment. There is no significant budgetary incentive to remove these units from Korea unless they are to be demobilized and removed from the U.S. force structure, for it would cost at least as much to maintain them in the United States as in Korea. Keeping them where they are would almost certainly continue to deter Kim Il-sung from attacking South Korea and would be strongly supported by both the government and the opposition in that country. It would reassure the Japanese and minimize the danger that the South Koreans would feel impelled to develop nuclear weapons. It would also tend to restrain the arms competition between the two Koreas. Unless tension between the two Koreas were to lessen, withdrawing the forces would not contribute to the achievement of U.S. objectives toward the Soviet Union and China; on the contrary, if the action made conflict in Korea more likely it would increase the risk of a military confrontation with these nations.

It is questionable, however, whether political support for the indefinite continuance of U.S. forces in South Korea—particularly ground forces in forward positions where they would be almost automatically involved were a conflict to break out—will continue to exist in the United States. It would be prudent to hedge against the erosion of that political support by proceeding as quickly as possible to strengthen the military forces of the Republic of Korea in a planned way, so that the withdrawal of U.S. *ground* forces three or four years from now would not significantly weaken the deterrent against a North Korean attack, even a blitzkrieg against Seoul.

The possibility of renewed political disturbance in South Korea, more repression by the government, and a consequent further decline in the number of Americans willing to see U.S. forces remain in South Korea makes more urgent the need to strengthen South Korean defenses. However, although the South Korean government should be made aware that further suppression of its noncommunist critics will diminish the amount of support it can expect to receive from the United States, any decision to withdraw U.S. forces should be based on a judgment concerning its effect on the likelihood of conflict rather than its effect on South Korean domestic politics.

A plan for the future reduction of U.S. forces in South Korea based on the strengthening of South Korean forces would have several advantages. It could be worked out in agreement with Park Chung-hee, who has said he expects South Korea to be self-sufficient militarily within four or five years. Such a plan also would be less likely to disturb the Japanese than a withdrawal on short notice brought about by political pressure in the United States. And it would be easier to maintain political support in the United States for the continued presence of some U.S. forces in Korea as long as may be necessary if South Korean forces were stronger than they are today and more confident that they could by themselves repel the invaders; U.S. forces could be held in reserve to be used only if the South Koreans were in danger of being defeated. Helping South Korea to attain this degree of military self-sufficiency is a realistic goal, given that country's size, its present military strength, and its economic power, present and potential.

A partial withdrawal of U.S. forces need not dangerously increase the likelihood that North Korea would launch a large-scale attack if it is accompanied by appropriate strengthening of South Korean forces. A carefully planned reduction, known to be carried out in cooperation with South Korea and in consultation with Japan, should not adversely affect either the stability of South Korea or U.S. relations with that country and Japan. The implications of alternative forms of partial withdrawal will be discussed below.

It could be argued that partial withdrawal, especially withdrawal of U.S. tactical nuclear weapons in South Korea, would increase the risk of the South Koreans' deciding they had to acquire their own nuclear weapons. There is little doubt that a decision to withdraw all U.S. forces despite strong South Korean objections would push them rapidly in this direction. Nuclear weapons in South Korean hands are clearly not in the U.S. interest. North Korea would feel bound to acquire them also; the shock to the Japanese would be profound; and hopes for maintaining a stable, low-tension equilibrium in Northeast Asia would be seriously undermined. But a partial withdrawal, carefully worked out with the South Koreans in advance and related to a program of building up their strength in conventional weapons, would be unlikely to significantly affect the pace at which they would in any case work toward improving their capability to produce nuclear weapons. Their progress can be slowed, though probably not halted, if the United States declares its adamant opposition to the acquisition of nuclear weapons by South Korea and takes every action available to it to interfere with South Korea's diverting its nuclear facilities to other than peaceful uses. The United States has substantial leverage because it controls the supply of enriched uranium to South Korea's power industry, it is the primary supplier of military equipment and spare parts to South Korea's armed forces, and no other nation is capable of giving South Korea the backing it requires to counter Soviet and Chinese backing of North Korea. For a long time to come, a cooperative relation with the United States is likely to be more important to South Koreans than acquiring nuclear weapons.

A Long-Term Policy

A plan for partial withdrawal of U.S. forces should be designed not only to meet the mid-term goals of deterring conflict and maintaining American political support for keeping some U.S. forces in South Korea, but also as part of a long-term policy aimed at lowering tension and diminishing the risk of war on the Korean peninsula. Tension can only be lessened if Kim Il-sung becomes convinced that his current hard-line policy cannot succeed—only a change in his policy would permit the beginning of genuine negotiations with South Korea on a step-by-step establishment of relations between North and South Korea. So drastic a change cannot be expected soon. Hence the United States must have a policy concerning its forces in South Korea that will be tenable for a good many years: no withdrawals for the next two years or so; thereafter, planned withdrawals worked out in agreement with South Korea and Japan; and eventual total withdrawal conditioned on substantial progress in negotiations between the two Koreas, reciprocal recognition of the two Koreas by the four big powers, and the entry of both Koreas into the United Nations.

The American political support necessary to sustain such a long-term policy will in part depend on halting the increasing repression of human rights in South Korea. The majority of Americans would probably grant that tight security and some limitations of constitutional democracy are inevitable in a state under siege like South Korea, but blatant and excessive acts of repression such as the abduction of opposition leader Kim Tae-chung from Tokyo cannot help but weaken American and Japanese support for Park Chung-hee's government.

The United States will have more influence on Park's actions if it maintains a significant combat force in Korea than if it withdraws all its forces as a protest against the South Korean government's repressive measures. Such a move would be widely regarded as a step in American disengagement from the defense commitment to South Korea, and the repercussions could be serious. The initial effect might be unifying, in generating a common perception of heightened danger, as occurred after the fall of the South Vietnamese government. But the action would probably eliminate any moderating influence the United States might have had on Park's behavior, and he might adopt still stronger measures to stifle opposition. It is significant that those who oppose Park also oppose the withdrawal of U.S. forces; this suggests that they feel their position would not improve if these forces left. Withdrawal despite the strong opposition of the South Korean government would alarm the Japanese government, which would see the action as increasing instability and the danger of war in the Korean peninsula as well as raising questions concerning the ultimate intentions of the United States toward its security commitment to Japan.

It would be important in carrying out a long-term policy of this kind not to provide arms to South Korea in quantities that would upset the military balance, cause North Korea to exert successful pressure on China and the Soviet Union for more weapons, and thus accelerate the arms race on the peninsula. Augmenting the military strength of North Korea and South Korea at a rapid rate would perpetuate the inherent instability caused by the obsession of both Koreas with military power and increase the danger that incidents might escalate into large-scale warfare not intended by either party. An excessive flow of arms to the South Korean armed forces seems unlikely, however, in view of the pressure in Congress to hold down military aid programs and South Korea's own limited ability to purchase or manufacture weapons. The United States might further minimize the danger by seeking to reinforce the tacit understanding between the United States, China, and the USSR that the outbreak of war in Korea would be contrary to the interests of each of them. The United States could let China and the Soviet Union know that it would not provide certain types of advanced conventional weapons to South Korea provided they withheld comparable weapons from North Korea.

A carefully worked-out long-term policy along the above lines would be both practicable and consonant with broader U.S. interests in Northeast Asia—maintaining close relations with a lightly armed, nonnuclear Japan and avoiding military confrontation with the USSR or China. Partial withdrawal of U.S. forces, especially removing them from the front lines where they would automatically be involved in any large-scale conflict, would make it easier to maintain the political support needed in the United States to keep the remaining U.S. forces there. The U.S. determination to keep significant combat forces in South Korea until the danger of conflict between the two Koreas had declined would be understood and tacitly accepted by the Soviet Union and China and would reassure the Japanese government.

Alternative Withdrawal Plans

For reasons that will be discussed below, withdrawal of major elements of U.S. forces in South Korea should be considered in the following order: first, tactical nuclear weapons; second, ground forces; and third, air force units.

Withdrawal of Tactical Nuclear Weapons

The presence of tactical nuclear weapons abroad has come under congressional scrutiny, primarily because of concern that some may be vulnerable to seizure by terrorists.[1] One witness before a congressional subcommittee, citing press reports that nuclear warheads in South Korea had been carried by helicopter to positions near the demilitarized zone for training purposes, expressed fear that a nuclear accident might result.[2] The danger that nuclear weapons might be captured is remote as long as they are in the hands of sizable U.S. military units. Even if threatened with capture in a North Korean attack, they could be destroyed or made unusable; units that have tactical nuclear weapons in their custody are trained in this procedure. The questions that should be asked concerning tactical nuclear weapons in Korea are more fundamental: how essential are they to the defense of South Korea and what would be the political costs if they were used?

Tactical nuclear weapons were introduced into South Korea when a combined Chinese–North Korean attack seemed a possibility. A good case could be made for the military usefulness of such weapons in resisting the onslaught of forces heavily outnumbering the defenders. At present,

1. *Washington Post,* September 20, 1974; *New York Times,* September 22, 1974.
2. Dr. Stefan Leader, Center for Defense Information, *Our Commitments in Asia,* Hearings before the Subcommittee on East Asian and Pacific Affairs of the House Committee on Foreign Affairs, 93:2 (GPO, 1974), pp. 166–67.

however, when the possibility of direct Chinese military intervention is discounted, the need for tactical nuclear weapons against North Korean forces fighting alone is questionable. It is true that in the event of a surprise attack on Seoul they could make crossings of the Imjin River near Mun-san-ni almost prohibitively costly and could be used with devastating effect against the narrow approach routes to Seoul. But now that the Soviet Union is also well supplied with such weapons, their use against North Korea could lead the USSR to provide its ally with similar weapons. It would be far better to rely on conventional forces to halt a blitzkrieg on Seoul than to plan on using nuclear weapons, for not only could the Soviet Union cancel out the military advantage that sole possession of nuclear weapons would have conferred on the combined U.S.–South Korean forces, but there would also be heavy political costs attached to their first use by the United States.

Using nuclear weapons against North Korea would strengthen the view, already widely held in Asia, that the United States would use them against Asians but not against white adversaries. Moreover, the strong opposition of many Japanese to the use of U.S. bases in Japan to support military operations in Korea would be greatly intensified. Because the Japanese are the only people to have suffered a nuclear bombing, emotions would run high and the damage to U.S. relations with Japan would be severe. The United States would be condemned throughout the world for being the first nation in over thirty years to break the barrier between conventional and nuclear weapons, and new impetus would be given to nuclear prolifer-ation.

It can be argued that the weapons should be left in South Korea as a deterrent, even though a decision had been reached not to use them. As long as they were there, Kim Il-sung could never count on their not being used. The United States could thus have the best of both worlds—gaining their deterrent value at only slight, if any, net political disadvantage while avoiding the high political cost of actually using them by being prepared to withdraw or destroy them if conflict occurred. This would be a risky course of action, however, for while they are in South Korea, there is the danger that military planners, relying too heavily on the expectation of being able to use them in an emergency, will neglect to do everything necessary to prepare the forces defending South Korea to meet an attack with conventional weapons only. Moreover, to diminish the danger that nuclear weapons will again be used in warfare, it is highly desirable to re-duce to a minimum situations in which nuclear weapons are relied on to deter or defeat an attack by conventional forces. Korea is a place where this could be done at relatively low risk.

Of course, the withdrawal of tactical nuclear warheads by the United States would have a psychological effect on both Koreas, somewhat diminishing the deterrent effect of the remaining U.S. forces and increasing doubt in South Korea about the reliability of the U.S. commitment. But the effect on the Japanese would probably be, on balance, favorable. Not even the Japanese government, which favors keeping U.S. forces in South Korea, would be likely to object to the withdrawal of nuclear warheads.

If the military outlook changed and, for example, Chinese military intervention in Korea appeared likely or the Russians were known to have placed tactical nuclear weapons in North Korea, U.S. warheads could be returned to South Korea quickly. But so long as there appears to be no overriding military requirement for them, the political reasons for taking them out are persuasive. They should not be removed within the next two years, but as soon as political conditions in East Asia permit a review of alternatives to the present level of U.S. forces in South Korea, they should be withdrawn.

Repositioning the U.S. 2nd Division

The bulk of the U.S. 2nd Division is based between Seoul and the DMZ, helping defend the most critical portion of the front, the approach route to Seoul. The principal advantage of having U.S. ground forces in this position is that it emphasizes the determination of the United States to fulfill its commitment to South Korea by keeping forces where they would be almost automatically involved at an early stage of the resistance to an attack from the north. The effect is to maximize both deterrence of North Korea and South Korean confidence in the United States. The fact that the division is positioned to defend against the kind of attack the South Koreans most fear—a blitzkrieg against Seoul—increases the value attached by the South Korean government to its presence there.

In 1974 Congress approved a recommendation by the House Appropriations Committee[3] that the 2nd Division be withdrawn from its forward position north of Seoul and located well to the rear. The committee took the view that repositioning the division in this manner would prevent its almost inevitable involvement in defending against a major North Korean

3. *Department of Defense Appropriation Bill 1975,* Report 93-1255 of the House Committee on Appropriations (to accompany H.R. 16243), 93:2 (GPO, 1974), p. 38.

attack and give the U.S. government time to consider whether intervention by U.S. ground forces was necessary. It recommended conversion of the division into a genuine reserve force for use as needed either in Korea or elsewhere in the Pacific theater. The committee further recommended that if the division were not so repositioned it be withdrawn entirely from South Korea beginning in 1976.

The Department of Defense opposes moving the 2nd Division back, partly because relocating it would be very costly and training areas comparable to those it now has would be difficult to obtain.[4] Requisitioning the needed land from farmers would create political difficulties for the South Korean government. Moreover, if the division were to be converted into a reserve force available for use outside Korea, the individual Korean soldiers now serving as "Korean Augmentation to the U.S. Army" would have to be replaced. Until recently these Korean soldiers constituted about 20 percent of the personnel of the division, and although some are being replaced, Defense is reluctant, mainly for budgetary reasons, to remove them all. The department argues that if a crisis arose and it was decided that U.S. forces should not be involved, the division could be pulled back from its present position. But such a withdrawal when attack was imminent or under way would be so damaging to South Korean morale that it hardly seems a practicable course of action.

Repositioning the 2nd Division to the rear, by making it easier to keep U.S. ground forces out of a conflict if they were not needed, would help maintain political support for keeping U.S. forces in South Korea. The deterrent effect of the U.S. military presence would be somewhat impaired, but less so than if the division were completely withdrawn. It is doubtful, however, that the advantages would outweigh the costs of repositioning unless the division remained many more years in South Korea, as it might be expected to do if it became the mobile theater reserve force recommended by Congress. But is there a strategic need for a mobile theater reserve? What kind of contingency in East Asia outside of Korea would require intervention by a full U.S. division—a division, moreover, stationed in Korea rather than in Hawaii or elsewhere in the United States? Is such a contingency conceivable in Southeast Asia or Taiwan? The rationale is not readily apparent. A survey of possible contingencies is beyond the scope of this study; all that needs to be said here is that the

---

4. *Department of Defense Appropriations for 1976*, Hearings before a subcommittee of the House Committee on Appropriations, 94:1, pt. 1 (GPO, 1975), pp. 357–59.

United States should not rush into the costly enterprise of making the 2nd Division over into a mobile reserve without a persuasive rationale supporting the need for such a unit.

It is also doubtful that moving the 2nd Division to the rear, but keeping it in Korea, would be a satisfactory first step in a long-term U.S. policy, unless the rear position were regarded as a halfway house toward total withdrawal. But that too would be costly; the funds spent on relocation would be better spent on planned strengthening of the South Korean forces, with the 2nd Division left where it is, providing maximum deterrence, until it can be withdrawn from Korea altogether.

Withdrawal of U.S. Ground Forces

Thus a long-term policy for Korea, to attract adequate support from the American people, should be based on a plan to withdraw U.S. ground forces entirely but gradually from South Korea while its own forces are being strengthened. Although actual withdrawal should not begin for two years, planning for it could begin now.

Withdrawal might begin with the smaller auxiliary units. The House Appropriations Committee recommended that the 38th Air Defense Artillery Brigade (except for its Chaparral/Vulcan antiaircraft battalion) be broken up and its Hawk and Nike-Hercules missiles and associated equipment be transferred to the Koreans. It also recommended that the 4th Missile Command (presumably with its Sergeant and Honest John nuclear-capable missiles) be withdrawn from Korea. Finally, it recommended a reduction in miscellaneous administrative and logistic support units, including transfer to the Koreans of full responsibility for the operation of the military port of Pusan. This proposed transfer of most of the air defense artillery and some of the logistic functions now handled by Americans would accord with a policy of assisting South Korea to become more self-reliant.

A program for strengthening the South Korean forces to permit the withdrawal of the U.S. 2nd Division should include provision by the United States of some of the weapons most useful to the South Koreans. Precision-guided missiles, which played such an important role in the recent war in the Middle East, would be highly effective against North Korean tanks and self-propelled artillery massed in an effort to break through South Korean lines. There is need for additional artillery and air defense equipment as well. The goal should be to give South Korea the capability to deal a devastating blow at a blitzkrieg against Seoul or an attempt to break through South Korean lines elsewhere so that the withdrawal of the U.S. division would neither weaken South Korean self-confidence nor tempt Kim Il-sung to take adventurous action. In view of the probable limitations on the U.S. global military aid program, much of the equipment needed probably would have to be purchased by Seoul for cash, but the South Koreans should be in a position to make such expenditures if world economic recovery occurs in the next year or so.

Under the long-term policy proposed here, U.S. air units would remain in South Korea after the withdrawal of U.S. ground forces. A program to build up the South Korean air force to a strength comparable to North Korea's could therefore be carried out over a longer period of time than the program to strengthen the ground forces. The latter would receive priority in the allocation of funds. The expansion of the air force could proceed at a pace that would not delay the acquisition of ground force equipment.

Planning the withdrawal of the U.S. 2nd Division from South Korea will have to include methods for transferring operational control of Korean forces from American to Korean commanders. The system of giving operational control of Korean forces to Americans originated in the UN Command structure but does not necessarily depend on the continuation of the UN Command. U.S. operational control could be perpetuated if U.S. forces remained in South Korea under bilateral agreements even if the UN Command were abolished.

U.S. operational command makes for greater efficiency than separate headquarters for U.S. and Korean forces linked only by liaison. It enables American officers to be extensively informed about the condition and activities of Korean forces and to participate in major decisions. It is an effective way of being prepared to deal with any conflict in which large numbers of U.S. forces might participate. The system also has certain political advantages. The intermingling of Americans and Koreans in the defense system not only improves mutual understanding but also bolsters the confidence of the Korean military in the determination of the United States to participate in the defense of South Korea. And the presence of Americans in the command structure means that they receive prompt intelligence concerning clashes between North Korean and South Korean units—particularly sea and air clashes—and can exert a moderating influence when necessary to prevent overreaction and the escalation of such incidents into more serious combat.

But it would be politically undesirable for the United States to retain operational control when it was in the process of withdrawing its last major ground force unit from South Korea. This would run counter to the trend toward military self-sufficiency in South Korea and to efforts by the South Korean government to strengthen its international position. It would lend credence to Kim Il-sung's taunts that Park Chung-hee is a puppet of the United States.

Withdrawal of All U.S. Forces

The U.S. air force wing should not be withdrawn from South Korea, even after the South Korean air force has been built up to the level of the North Korean air force, until the tension and danger of hostilities between the two Koreas is substantially lessened. Total U.S. withdrawal from South Korea would probably convince all governments concerned that the United States was unlikely to intervene militarily in the event of a conflict in Korea, whatever the U.S. government might say about its determination to fulfill its defense commitment. They could not rule out entirely the return of U.S. forces, as happened in 1950, but times have changed and the refusal of the United States to become militarily reinvolved in South Vietnam doubtless would be regarded as a better precedent for the late 1970s than U.S. behavior in 1950.

Total withdrawal would increase the risk that Kim Il-sung would feel emboldened to attack South Korea, would reduce the willingness and ability of China and the USSR to restrain him, would undermine the confidence of South Koreans, and would cause the Japanese to question the firmness of the U.S. commitment to Japan. There is no satisfactory substitute for a significant U.S. combat force stationed in Korea as an earnest of U.S. intentions. The decision to remove all U.S. forces should be made only when other changes in and around Korea have so reduced the risk of renewed conflict there that their presence is generally recognized in South Korea and Japan as no longer being necessary. The most persuasive indicators that this time had arrived would be genuine progress in peaceful interaction between the two Koreas, including trade and travel back and forth, the reciprocal recognition of North and South Korea by all four big powers, and the entry of both Koreas into the United Nations.